INDOLOGY

MOTILAL BANARSIDASS PUBLISHERS
DELHI

2003

NARSIDASS

SHERS

VEDIC HERMENEUTICS

VEDIC HERMENEUTICS

श्रुत्यर्थपर्यालोचना

K. SATCHIDANANDA MURTY

SHRI LAL BAHADUR SHASTRI
RASHTRIYA SANSKRIT VIDYAPEETHA
NEW DELHI

in association with
MOTILAL BANARSIDASS PUBLISHERS
PRIVATE LIMITED • DELHI

First Edition: Delhi, 1993

ISBN: 81-208-1105-4

Published by
SHRI LAL BAHADUR SHASTRI RASHTRIYA SANSKRIT VIDYAPEETHA
NEW DELHI

in association with
MOTILAL BANARSIDASS PUBLISHERS PVT. LTD.
DELHI

Available at:
MOTILAL BANARSIDASS
41 U.A. Bungalow Road, Jawahar Nagar, Delhi 110 007
120 Royapettah High Road, Mylapore, Madras 600 004
16 St. Mark's Road, Bangalore 560 001
Ashok Rajpath, Patna 800 004
Chowk, Varanasi 221 001

PRINTED IN INDIA
BY JAINENDRA PRAKASH JAIN AT SHRI JAINENDRA PRESS,
A-45 NARAINA INDUSTRIAL AREA, PHASE I, NEW DELHI 110 028

नानाभाषाविबुधाय, विविधवाङ्मय-विचक्षणाय
बहुसंमतनयनिष्णाताय
भारतप्रधानमन्त्रिणे,
तत्रभवते पामुलपर्ति वेंकट नरसिंहराव महोदयाय,
तदनुमत्या उपायनीकरोति ।

वसन्तपञ्चमी, 28 जनवरी 1993 के. सच्चिदानन्द मूर्तिः
राष्ट्रिय माघः 8, 1914

विशुद्धज्ञानदेहाय त्रिवेदीदिव्यचक्षुषे ।
श्रेयःप्राप्तिनिमित्ताय नमः सोमार्धधारिणे ॥

Pure knowledge constitutes His body and the three Vedas His divine eyes. He is the cause of the attainment of the supreme good. He wears the crescent moon. My obeisance to Him.

—Kumārila, *Ślokavārttika*

शब्दब्रह्मेति यच्चेदं शास्त्रं वेदाख्यमुच्यते ।
तदप्यधिष्ठितं सर्वमेकेन परमात्मना ॥

All this sacred lore named the Veda, which is also said to be Brahman in the form of words, is established and inspired by the one Supreme Self.

—Kumārila, *Tantravārttika*

प्राक्कथन

"श्रुत्यर्थपर्यालोचना" के रूप में यह लघुकाय, परन्तु अतिशय सारगर्भित गंभीरार्थ-संपन्न कृति तीन अध्यायों में सम्पूर्ण होती है। प्रथम अध्याय का पहला भाग वेद के लक्षण और विषय का विवेचन करता है। कात्यायन, आपस्तम्ब, बोधायन, शबर इत्यादि आचार्यों का मत था कि मन्त्र और ब्राह्मण दोनों मिलकर वेद है। यास्क और पाणिनि ने निगम एवं ब्राह्मणों में भेद को स्वीकार किया और कुछ विद्वानों ने उन्नीसवीं शताब्दी में मन्त्र संहिताओं को वेद माना। उसके बाद अन्य मनीषियों ने भी उनका अनुकरण किया। सायणाचार्य ने वेद के तीन लक्षण उद्धृत किये हैं :

"मन्त्र ब्राह्मण शब्द राशि वेद है।"

"परम पुरुषार्थ प्राप्त करने का अलौकिक साधन वेद है।"

"इष्ट प्राप्ति और अनिष्ट परिहार का अलौकिक उपाय वेद है।"

सायणाचार्य आरण्यक और उपनिषदों को भी वेद मानते हैं। मन्त्र ब्राह्मणों को वेद मानते हुए मधुसूदन सरस्वती ने ब्राह्मणों में विधि, अर्थवाद और उनसे विलक्षण वेदान्त वाक्यों का भी समावेश किया है। उदयनाचार्य ने वेद के दो भाग किये हैं-भव्यार्थ भाग (साध्यार्थ भाग या क्रिया भाग) और भूतार्थ भाग (सिद्धार्थ भाग)।

पूर्ववर्ती वेद के अनुयायी तथा प्रधान वैदिक परम्परा में आस्था रखने वाले अर्वाचीन मनीषियों की भावना है कि धर्म और ब्रह्म केवल एकमात्र वेद से ही जाने जा सकते हैं। इन दोनों का अनन्यलभ्य होने के कारण वेद-विषयत्व है। प्रधान वैदिक परम्परा का अभिप्राय है-जो मीमांसक, वेदान्ती, नैयायिक, तथा स्मृति, तथा इतिहास पुराण आदि के द्वारा समादृत है।

वेद और पुराणों का क्या सम्बन्ध है? क्या उनमें विरोध सम्भव है? मीमांसक आदि ने इसके बारे में क्या प्रतिपादित किया है? इन सब पर भी आलोचना की गई है।

आगे चलकर वेदार्थ जानने का महत्त्व सप्रमाण सिद्ध किया गया है–वेद की अनेक व्याख्याओं की रचना अति प्राचीन काल से आज तक किस प्रकार सम्भव हो रही है ? वेदों की प्रामाणिकता और उपादेयता का निश्चय कैसे किया जा सकता है ? वेद में क्या कतिपय निण्य (रहस्यात्मक) वचन हैं ? क्या उसमें उच्चावच अभिप्राय है ? क्या यह सत्य है–"त्रयोऽर्था: सर्ववेदेषु" ? वास्तव में कोई भी पवित्र धर्म ग्रन्थ अक्षरश: सम्पूर्णतया निर्दोष हो सकता है क्या ?

इसी अध्याय में वेद के अध्ययन के अधिकार से सम्बद्ध वाद-विवादों की समीक्षा है । वेद अपने को सार्वकालिक और सार्वजनीन घोषित करता है । वह देश, जाति, वर्ण, वर्ग, लिंग आदि के आधार पर अपने अध्ययन का निषेध नहीं करता । कुछ स्मृतियों में इस तरह के निषेध वाक्य हैं, लेकिन उस तरह के वाक्यों में अधिक गहनता और गम्भीरता के दर्शन नहीं होते । श्रुति विश्व के समस्त मानवों के हित के लिए देदीप्यमान दिव्य वाणी है । सभी लोग जिनकी भी कामना और सामर्थ्य है, वे वेद का अध्ययन-अध्यापन और प्रचार कर सकते हैं, करते हैं, कर रहे हैं और भविष्य में भी करेंगे । लेखक का यह अति सूक्ष्म विवेचन है ।

द्वितीय अध्याय इस विवाद से प्रारम्भ होता है–क्या संहिता ही वेद है या ब्राह्मण उपनिषद् मात्र ही वेद है ? या केवल उपनिषद् ही हमारे लिये मान्य हैं ? सिद्धान्त रूप से लेखक का मंतव्य है कि निरुक्त, विभिन्न भाष्य ग्रन्थ, षड्दर्शन, शैव, वैष्णव, आदि सम्प्रदाय, शंकर, रामानुज, मध्व आदि परम आचार्यों, सायण, राघवेन्द्र, हरदत्त आदि वेद भाष्य एवं टीकाकारों तथा स्मृति, इतिहास और पुराणों ने जिसको वेद मान कर गम्भीरता के साथ जिसकी व्याख्या की है, वही यथार्थ में वेद है । यह वाङ्मय कई हजार वर्षों से करोड़ों व्यक्तियों के मानस पर प्रभाव प्रतिष्ठित करता रहा है । उसके अर्थ और तात्पर्य को सहानुभव, ससंवेदन, समग्रता, अखण्डता में स्वीकार कर अति प्राचीन काल से उसके अर्थबोध और व्याख्यान के लिए जिन नियमों और सूत्रों का उपयोग हुआ है, उन्हीं के द्वारा हम उसके अर्थ और तात्पर्य को समझें, यह आवश्यक है । उसके बाद हम चाहें तो भले ही उससे असहमत हो सकते हैं । इसका खण्डन या परित्याग कर सकते हैं । इसके साथ-साथ इसी भाग में अज्ञातज्ञापनार्थ प्रवृत्त शास्त्र के तात्पर्यभूत मुख्य अर्थ या प्रधान अर्थ का निश्चय किस प्रकार करना चाहिए, इसकी चर्चा भी है । सम्यक् अन्वय अथवा सम्यक्त्व का क्या तात्पर्य है ? धर्मराज का निम्नलिखित तात्पर्य लक्षण शताब्दियों के चिन्तन की परिणति है–

"तत्प्रतीतिजननयोग्यत्वम्, तदितरप्रतीतीच्छया अनुच्चरितत्वम् ।"

इस सन्दर्भ में प्रकरणार्थ विचार में षड्लिंग, उपक्रम, पराक्रम, अपच्छेद-न्याय, शास्त्र का आरम्भ और अन्त, भिन्न शाखाओं के मध्य संवाद की अपेक्षा, व्युत्पत्ति द्वारा शब्द का ज्ञान आदि का दिङ्मात्र रूप में निर्देश किया गया है । परन्तु यह ध्यान रखना चाहिए कि जिस प्रकार वैज्ञानिक चिन्तनपरक पुरुष बुद्धि जिस को मुख्य या महत्त्वपूर्ण मानती है और उसी पर अधिक निर्भर करती है, वही स्थिति अर्थावगति और तात्पर्य निर्णय में भी है ।

आगे चलकर निरुक्त के आधार पर स्थापित किया गया है कि जिन्होंने धर्म का साक्षात्कार किया है, उन्हें ऋषि कहा जाता है । वास्तव में जब ऋषि नहीं होते, तब तर्क ही ऋषि है । मन्त्रार्थ-चिन्तन से जो अभ्यूहित होता है वही आर्ष है । श्रुति के आधार पर तर्क से जो अभ्यूहित होता है, वह आर्ष ही है । निरुक्त ने यह भी स्पष्ट किया है कि मन्त्र पृथक्त्वेन नहीं, अपितु समग्रतया निर्वचनीय हैं । दुर्गाचार्य ने निरुक्त व्याख्यान में कहा है-वेद मन्त्रों को आधियज्ञिक, आधिदैविक या आध्यात्मिक ढंग से समझ सकते हैं, उनमें जितने अर्थ उपपाद्य हैं, वे सभी योज्य हैं, ऐसा कहने में कोई दोष नहीं है । स्कंद-महेश्वर का मत है -

"सब दर्शनों में सारे मंत्र योजनीय हैं ।'

यह सब व्याख्या स्वातन्त्र्य के "चार्टर" (शासनपत्र) के समान है ।

इसके अग्रिम भाग में यह दिखाने का प्रयास है कि वैदिक मत यौक्तिक है या तार्किक श्रद्धा । पारस्कर गृह्यसूत्र का वचन है-

"विधिर्विधेयस्तर्कश्च वेदः"

कुमारिल भट्टपाद के अनुसार मीमांसा-

"समस्तवैदिकतर्कोपसंहारात्मिका" है ।

उनकी बृहत् टीका में लिखा है, वयं तु अन्श्रद्धधानाः युक्तीः प्रार्थयामहे ।

वाचस्पति मिश्र ने न्यायवार्तिकतात्पर्यटीका में घोषणा की है-

"मीमांसासंज्ञिकस्तर्कः सर्ववेदसमुद्भवः"

भामती में तो उन्होंने कहा है-

'वेदान्तमीमांसा तावत् तर्क एव ।"

हाँ, उपादेय तर्क श्रुति द्वारा प्रतिष्ठित श्रुति के अनुकूल और श्रुति से अविरोधी होता है, अन्ध या शुष्क नहीं हो सकता । सभी मीमांसक और वेदान्तियों और अन्य दार्शनिकों ने एकमत होकर कहा है–श्रुति में प्रत्यक्ष अनुमान आदि प्रमाणों के विरुद्ध कुछ भी नहीं है ।

"दृष्ट विषय में आगम की अन्वेषणा नहीं है" (शंकराचार्य)
"प्रत्यक्ष पदार्थग्राही है, शास्त्र प्रत्यक्ष से अपरिच्छेद्य है" (रामानुजाचार्य)
"अनुभवविरोध में आगम का प्रामाण्य नहीं है" (मध्वाचार्य)

इन सब वाक्यों के अनुवाद और निर्दिष्ट स्थल इस अध्याय और टिप्पणियों में प्रस्तुत हैं ।

"इतिहासपुराणाभ्यां वेदं समुपबृंहयेत्"–यह महाभारत और नारदीय पुराण का वचन है । यह भी कहा गया है–

"प्रायेण पूर्वभागार्थो धर्मशास्त्रेण कथ्यते,
इतिहासपुराणाभ्यां वेदान्तार्थः प्रकाश्यते ।"

इस अध्याय में निम्नलिखित विषयों पर भी विचार–विमर्श किया गया है:

वेद अपने आप के बारे में पूर्वोत्तर भागों में क्या कहते है ?

सूत्र, स्मृति साहित्य विभिन्न आचार्यों के ग्रन्थों में तथा न्यायवैशेषिक सांख्य व्याकरण आदि में वेद के विषय में क्या कहा गया है ?

पूर्वोत्तर मीमांसकों के अभिप्राय तो इस पुस्तक में स्थान–स्थान पर यत्र–तत्र बिखरे हुए हैं । मूल रूप से मनुस्मृति ने वेदार्थ का विवेचन किस प्रकार किया है तथा महाभारत, रामायण, भगवद्गीता आदि वेदार्थ किस रूप में प्रकाशित करते हैं, यह विस्तार से उपस्थापित है । भगवद्गीता को शंकराचार्य ने समस्त वेदार्थ-सारसंग्रह कहा है । सारे वेदान्ताचार्य, परम वैष्णव और परम माहेश्वर (अभिनवगुप्त) भी यही कहते हैं । इसलिए गीता में वेद के बारे में प्रकटित सभी विचार इस भाग में पूर्ण रूप से चर्चित हैं ।

इस अध्याय के अन्तिम भाग में उन उपस्थापित विषयों का उपसंहार करते हुए महाभारत की निम्नलिखित अति गहन समस्याओं और उनके समाधान के विवरण दिये गये हैं–

वेदवाद का अनुयुग ह्रास होता है, युगानुरूप धर्म भिन्न होते हैं, स्मृति वचन

सत्य हैं, वेद विश्वतोमुख है । आम्नाय वचन सत्य हैं । वेद आम्नाय वचन से पर हैं । वेद उनके तथा शास्त्रों के प्रामाण्य और अप्रामाण्य तथा परस्पर विरोधी वचनों के अर्थों के व्याख्यान से इस अध्याय की समाप्ति होती है ।

तीसरे अध्याय में वेदान्त का सिद्धान्त है : वेद का योनि ब्रह्म है, पर वह अपौरुषेय है, क्योंकि उसकी रचना में पुरुष का कर्तृत्त्व नहीं हैं । मीमांसा बताती है-वेद विश्व की भाँति अनादि है तथा उसका कर्त्ता न होने के कारण वह अपौरुषेय सिद्ध होता है । न्याय सर्वज्ञपूर्वकत्व और प्रवाह-नित्यत्व के आधार पर वेद का ईश्वर-कर्तृत्त्व सिद्ध करता है।

आचार्य श्री सच्चिदानन्द मूर्ति को इस विषय में केवल श्वेताश्वतरोपनिषद् और गीता के वचन शिरोधार्य हैं-"ईश्वरो वेदान् प्रहिणोति", ईश्वर वेदान्तकृत् और वेदविद् है । वे ऐसा भी समझते हैं कि लौकिक प्रमाणों से अलभ्य ज्ञान ही वेद से परिज्ञात हो सकता है ।

इससे यह निगमन होता है कि वेद लौकिक ज्ञान नहीं देते हैं क्योंकि वे अन्य प्रमाणों से लभ्य ज्ञान की पुनरुक्ति नहीं करेंगे । इसलिए वेद में इतिहास, विज्ञान (साइन्स) आदि लौकिक ज्ञान का अन्वेषण करना "कौपीनाच्छादनप्राया वांछा कल्पद्रुमादपि" जैसा है । वास्तव में श्रुति तो अनन्यलभ्य धर्म और ब्रह्म विषयक ज्ञान देने के लिए है । इससे आगे चलकर संहिता-ब्राह्मण-उपनिषदों में यज्ञ के जो अर्थ दिये गये हैं, उनकी पर्यालोचना कर उनका परिष्कृत परमार्थ निश्चय करने का प्रयत्न किया गया है ।

आचार्य मूर्ति का प्रतिपादन है कि इतिहास-पुराणों से यह स्पष्ट होता है कि एक ही वेद का सत्यवती पुत्र ने विव्यास या विभजन किया । चारों वेदों का समन्वयपूर्वक मनन करने से उनकी एकवाक्यता प्रतीत होती है । ऋग्वेद सत्तत्त्व का वर्णन करता है, यजुर्वेद श्रेष्ठतम कर्म (यज्ञ) का उपदेश देता है । सामवेद ऋचाओं का गान करता है । आचार्य सायण के शब्दों में सब वेदों का सार होने के कारण अथर्ववेद श्रेष्ठ है । गोपथ आदि ब्राह्मण इसको ब्रह्म वेद कहते हैं । अद्वैत के पुरुष-ब्रह्म से ऐक्य का अथर्ववेद ने जिस प्रकार प्रतिपादन किया है-और किसी वेद ने नहीं । जयन्त भट्ट भी इस श्रेष्ठता को स्वीकार करते हैं । अथर्ववेद यह उद्घोषणा करता है कि विद्वान् इस पुरुष को ही ब्रह्म मानते हैं । पुरुष में ही ब्रह्म को पहचानना चाहिए । ब्रह्मविद् अपने ही शरीर में स्थित यक्ष को अकाम, धीर, रसतृप्त, अमृत, स्वयंभू, अजर, युवा आत्मा जानकर मृत्यु से नहीं डरते, जिसे

तीव्र जिज्ञासा है, वह जिसमें विश्व एक रूप बना है, उसके परम तत्त्व के रहस्य का अवलोकन करता है ।

वेद वाक्यों से स्पष्ट है कि सब वेदों का तात्पर्य एक ही है-

सर्वे वेदा यत्रैकं भवन्ति,
सर्वे वेदा यत्पदमामनंति ।

सभी वेदवेत्ताओं का मत भी यही है । कुमारिल और प्रभाकर का अभिप्राय है –

मीमांसा केवल काम्यकर्मों का यांत्रिक अनुष्ठान का विधान करने वाला शास्त्र नहीं है । वह तो ईश्वर को अर्पित करने की बुद्धि से निष्काम भावना के निर्वहण के द्वारा मृदितकषाय होकर, वेदान्त निषेवण कर परमार्थ लाभ करने का उपदेश देता है । शब्द ब्रह्म परमात्मा से अधिष्ठित है । (कुमारिल)

आत्म विषय में सारा वेद उपयुक्त है एवं ज्ञानकाण्ड का कर्म काण्ड से ऐकमत्य है (शंकराचार्य) ।

सारे वेद परब्रह्मभूत नारायण का स्वरुप, आराधना के प्रकार तथा आराधना के फल का बोध कराते हैं (रामानुजाचार्य)

सब वेद विष्णुपरक ही हैं (मध्वाचार्य)

सब वेदों से केवल ब्रह्म ही अधिगम्य है (सायणाचार्य) ।

वेद केवल ईश्वर को प्रकाशित करता है (हरदत्त शिवाचार्य)

इस पुस्तक के अन्तिम अध्याय में यह सब विद्वतापूर्ण शैली में आचार्य श्री के॰ सच्चिदानंद मूर्ति ने प्रतिपादित किया है । इसका प्रकाशन विद्यापीठ के लिये गरिमा का विषय है । इसका पहला कारण यह है कि यह वेदों के अर्थ की पर्यालोचना से सम्बद्ध है । भारतीय वाङ्मय में वेदों का जो मौलिक और उत्कृष्टतम स्थान है उससे सारा संसार सुपरिचित है । इसलिए वेद के अर्थ पर ग्रन्थ की प्रस्तुति अपने आप में एक उपलब्धि है । दूसरा कारण यह है कि इसके लेखक वर्तमान युग की भारतीय मनीषा की एक श्रेष्ठ और वरिष्ठतम विभूति हैं जो आचार्य श्री के॰ सच्चिदानंद मूर्ति के नाम से समस्त विश्व में मानविकी विद्याओं के महनीय विशेषज्ञ के रुप में सुप्रतिष्ठित हैं । उनके व्यक्तित्व और कृतित्व की शब्दों में अभिव्यक्ति सम्भव नहीं है क्योंकि उनका समस्त जीवन ज्ञान की विविध विधाओं से ओतप्रोत है । एक ओर दर्शन शास्त्र के महान् आचार्य के रूप में तो दूसरी ओर कुलपति और विश्वविद्यालय अनुदान आयोग के उपाध्यक्ष, अखिल भारतीय दर्शन परिषद् और दर्शन कांग्रेस के सभापति, अन्तर्राष्ट्रिय बौद्ध विद्या सम्मेलन और आदि

शंकराचार्य की राष्ट्रीय समितियों के मूल पुरुष एवं भारतीय विद्याओं के सार्वदेशिक स्वरुप की पुनः प्रतिष्ठा के लिए संस्थापित राष्ट्रिय समिति के अध्यक्ष के रूप में उनकी सेवायें समस्त विश्व में समादृत हैं। राष्ट्रपति की ओर से पद्म-भूषण और भारत, जर्मनी, रूस, बल्गारिया आदि के विश्वविद्यालयों द्वारा दी गई विभिन्न मानद उपाधियों से आचार्य मूर्ति शारदा के वरद पुत्र के रूप में सम्मानित किये गये हैं। उनमें अद्वैत और बौद्ध तत्त्व ज्ञान, प्राच्य और पाश्चात्य दर्शन एक साथ आश्रय प्राप्त कर विकसित हुए हैं, यह उनके व्यक्तित्व की एक अनुपम विशेषता है। शारदापीठ शृंगेरी के जगद्गुरु शंकराचार्य ने उनको "विद्यासागर" की उपाधि से अलंकृत कर समस्त सम्मान परम्परा को एक प्रकार से रत्नजड़ित कर दिया है। महामहोपाध्याय श्री पट्टाभिराम शास्त्री ने उनके साथ "नानाशास्त्रप्रक्षालितमतिवैभव" यह विशेषण लगाकर एक ही विशेषण में उनके पाण्डित्य की व्यापकता को साकार कर दिया है। स्वर्गीय डा॰ सुनीति कुमार चटर्जी, डा॰ सी॰ पी॰ रामास्वामी अय्यर जैसे इस राष्ट्र के महान् मनीषियों ने एक महान् लेखक, दार्शनिक और वाचस्पति के अभिनव स्वरुप के समान आचार्य मूर्ति की जो प्रशस्तियाँ आरम्भ की थीं, धीरे-धीरे उनकी शृंखला में सारे विश्व में एक पर एक कड़ी जुड़ती चली गई। इसी आशय के एक प्रतिफलित उदाहरण के रुप में भारतीय संस्कृति, इतिहास और तत्व ज्ञान के सम्माननीय विद्वान्, राजस्थान विश्वविद्यालय के पूर्व कुलपति डा॰ गोविन्द चन्द्र पाण्डेय ने आचार्य मूर्ति की प्रशस्ति-पद्यमाला को मैं इसी प्राक्कथन के साथ अलग पत्र पर प्रकाशित कर रहा हूँ।

संक्षेप में प्राच्य विद्या और संस्कृत से सम्बद्ध संस्थाओं के लिए उनका व्यक्तित्व इसलिए विशेष रूप से आदरणीय है कि उन्होंने ऊँचे-से-ऊँचे आसन पर विराजमान रहते हुए और आधुनिक से आधुनिक दार्शनिक तत्त्व चिन्तन में विशेषज्ञता धारण करते हुए भी संस्कृत के प्राचीन पंडितों का सदा सम्मान किया और स्वयं भी बहुत गम्भीरता के साथ संस्कृत में निहित दर्शनों का गहन अध्ययन और मनन किया। उन्होंने संस्कृत विद्वानों को आधुनिक धारा के साथ जोड़ने का भी प्रयास किया और आधुनिक विद्वानों में उनकी प्रतिष्ठा का संवर्धन किया। यह पारस्परिक आदान-प्रदान पद्धति का श्रीगणेश उनका ऐतिहासिक अवदान है। उनके परम्परागत ज्ञान के माहात्म्य के प्रति सारी विद्वन्मण्डली के सम्मान की अभिव्यक्ति ही वास्तव में सम्पूर्णानन्द संस्कृत विश्वविद्यालय, वाराणसी की मानद उपाधि "वाचस्पति" में होती है जो उनको 1980ई॰ में समर्पित की गई। एक कुशल अध्यापक, दृढ़

और सक्षम प्रशासक, नव-नव बौद्धिक जागृति के प्रवर्त्तक, नवीन-नवीन प्रतिभाओं, लेखकों और विद्वानों के मार्ग-दर्शक और संरक्षक के रुप में इस राष्ट्र में उनका स्थान अद्वितीय है । उनका व्यक्तित्व वैदुष्य, सरलता तथा सौजन्य का आकर है और हर छोटे से छोटे शिक्षक तथा विचारक को भी उनमें निकटतम आत्मीयता का अनुभव होता है और उनका सान्निध्य प्राप्त कर कृतकृत्य हो जाता है ।

इस प्रकार के महापुरुष की लेखनी द्वारा वेदों के अर्थ के विषय में की गई पर्यालोचना इसलिए भी महत्त्वपूर्ण है कि यह ज्ञान के साथ-साथ उनके समस्त जीवन के चिन्तन और अनुभव का प्रतिफलन है । इसके प्रकाशन का सौभाग्य उन्होंने विद्यापीठ को प्रदान किया, यह उनका एक प्रकार से इस संस्था और विशेषकर मुझ पर उनके व्यक्तिगत स्नेह और प्रसाद का परिणाम है । आचार्य मूर्ति विद्या, विनय और विवेक की साक्षात् प्रतिमा है । उनकी रचनाओं में सदा "नामूलं लिख्यते किंचित् नानपेक्षितमुच्यते" का अक्षरशः प्रतिफलन है । यह ग्रन्थ भी उनके सप्रमाण प्रतिपादन का निदर्शन है ।

भारतीय विद्याओं के विश्वविख्यात प्रकाशक मोतीलाल बनारसीदास जैसे प्रतिष्ठित संस्थान ने इसके प्रकाशन में सहयोग देने और इसके प्रसारण का दायित्व लिया है । वे तो विद्यापीठ और डा० मूर्ति से शाश्वत रूप से सम्बद्ध हैं । उनको आचार्य मूर्ति के अभिनन्दन ग्रन्थ (फ्रीडम, प्रोग्रेस एण्ड सोसायटी) और अन्य रचनाओं के भी प्रकाशन का सुयोग मिला है । उसी परम्परा में उन्होंने अपने जैनेन्द्र प्रेस के माध्यम से यह जो सुंदर सुरुचिपूर्ण प्रकाशन किया है, उसके लिए उनके प्रतिनिधि के रूप में श्री नरेन्द्र प्रकाश जैन हमारे धन्यवाद के पात्र हैं ।

उपरिलिखित संक्षिप्त निरूपण से इस ग्रन्थ की महत्ता का सहज ही में अनुमान लगाया जा सकता है । इस महत्त्वपूर्ण प्रकाशन से विश्वविद्यालय परिवार अत्यन्त हर्ष-प्रकर्ष का अनुभव कर रहा है ।

एक बार फिर आचार्य मूर्ति की विद्वत्ता के प्रति नमन करते हुए मैं यह ग्रन्थ इन्हीं शब्दों के साथ विश्व के बौद्धिक जगत् के समक्ष प्रस्तुत करता हूँ ।

महाशिवरात्रि
19 फरवरी, 1993 ई०

मण्डन मिश्र
कुलपति
श्री लालबहादुर शास्त्री
राष्ट्रिय संस्कृत विद्यापीठ,
नई दिल्ली

राज्ये विद्वत्सभायां जयति गुणगणैः सच्चिदानन्द मूर्तिः

निगमजलधिजातं रत्नजातं विचित्य
मतिविभवसमुत्थैर्युक्तिमुक्ताकलापैः ।
रचयति नवहारं देवतायै गिरां यः
स जयति बुधमध्ये सच्चिदानन्दमूर्तिः ॥

*

उभयजलधिचारी यस्य वैदुष्यपोतो
रविशशिसितकीर्तिप्रोतवस्त्रोत्पताकः ।
निखिलमनुजसाम्यप्रीतिसन्देशहारी
हृदि धृतहरिमूर्तिः सच्चिदानन्दमूर्तिः ॥

*

नीतिन्यायेतिहासप्रभृतिकृतमतिर्नैकशास्त्रप्रवीणः
प्राज्ञो वाग्मी सचेता अटति जनपदान् कोऽप्यपूर्वः परिव्राट् ।
सौम्यः स्निग्धः स्वभावादृजुमृदुमधुरः सत्यधर्मप्रतिष्ठो
राज्ये विद्वत्सभायां जयति गुणगणैः सच्चिदानन्दमूर्तिः ॥

गोविन्दचन्द्रपाण्डेयः *

* इतिहास, पुरातत्व, भारतीय विद्या, संस्कृति एवं तत्त्वज्ञान के विश्वविख्यात महामनीषी राजस्थान विश्वविद्यालय के पूर्व कुलपति

Having gathered the precious gems produced by the ocean that is the *Veda*, and taking up the clusters of pearls that are the rational arguments arising from his ample intellect, Satchidananda Murty makes a new garland for the goddess of learning. Varily he excels in the assembly of the learned.

The ship of his learning moves freely in both the oceans (eastern and western) with the sails woven of fame white as the sun and the moon, and unfurled as a flag. It carries the message of equality and love for all mankind. Satchidananda Murty keeps the form of Hari constantly in his heart.

He has perfectly grasped the sciences of philosophy, politics, history and the rest. He has mastered many sastras. He is a keen intellect, an eloquent speaker, a man of taste and sympathy. He has wandered in diverse climes, a Wandering Ascetic Teacher of an entirely new kind. He is mild and affectionate by nature, straight, kind and sweet. He takes his stand on Truth and Virtue. By his numerous qualities Satchidananda Murty excels as much in learned assemblies as in public office.

G. C. PANDE*

* An internationally known scholar in History, Archaeology, Indology, Culture and Philosophy and formerly Vice-Chancellor of Rajasthan University, Jaipur

PREFACE

I am neither a "Vedavratasnāta" (i.e., one who has "completed *one's* Vedic and scientific studies and *one's* vows"[1]), nor a "Vedapāraga" (i.e., "one thoroughly conversant with the Veda"[2]); I wonder how many of those who have written on the Veda in Western or modern Indian languages, or have translated it into them, have been such. I have been only endeavouring to dó upāsanā[3] of śruti-bhagavatī[4] for quite a long time: From the middle of the 30s to the beginning of the 40s one of my major preoccupations was to understand and elucidate the work which, according to the Vārāha-purāṇa, is "the three Vedas, ultimate bliss and united with the knowledge of the import of Reality"[5], and which, according to A.K. Coomaraswami, is a "compendium of all Vedic doctrines"[6], viz., the *Bhagavadgītā.*[7] As I have not so far succeeded in this task to my satisfaction, it still engrosses me and is likely to be life-long.[8] In the first half of the 40s I intensely studied the *Īśa,* the smallest, but one of the most profound and the only Upaniṣad which is to be found in the Saṁhitā portion.[9] Then, from the mid-40s to mid-50s I was obsessed with "śrutiprāmāṇyavicāra" (=thinking about the authority and validity of the Veda).[10] As I find I cannot be satiated by Vedārtha-cintana (meditation on the import of the Veda), however much I may indulge in it, I may never become free from this passion also. The results of my study of texts dealing with *Yajña* along with relevant sociological and anthropological literature, were published in 1973.[11]

One of the gratifying things I could do at Tirupati when I headed the S.V. University there (1975-78) was to make its

Oriental Institute prepare and publish in Telugu in 1978 a 'vivṛti' (explanation) of the first forty sūktas of the Ṛgveda, according to the bhāṣya of Madhvācārya and Rāghavendra Svāmī's *Mantrārthamañjarī* based on it. It contains word-by-word meaning (pratipadārtha) of every mantra, followed by its substance in simple prose, written by Dr. S.B. Raghunathacharyulu. It appeared with a 22-page Introduction by me. Thus was published for the first time in a modern language—a monotheistic interpretation of these sūktas according to the greatest Dvaita teachers.

When I was with the University Grants Commission (1986-89), one of my first acts was to help establish a centre for Vedic studies in a state university in the East of India, and later I could provide special assistance to promote Mīmāṁsā studies in a premier central university in the North. After sanctioning grants, as universities are autonomous, the UGC could *only* hope they would be utilised properly for purposes earmarked.

The chapters in this book and the notes of them will give an indication of some of the books I more often used. But I may mention that among the older works those of Yāska, Sāyaṇa and Ātmānanda, and among the modern those of Swami Dayananda Saraswati, Sri Aurobindo and T.V. Kapali Sastry were very helpful. I am indebted to the two epics and the *Śrīmadbhāgavata*, as well as to the writings of the great masters of Mīmāṁsā and Vedānta for enabling me to comprehend to some extent and assess however inadequately the purport of the Veda. Every modern Indian like me, who has used the Western editions and translations of the Veda and the monographs and articles on it by Western scholars, ought to be grateful for the immense benefit derived from them. Since the mid-80s I have used the Saṁhitā texts edited by Pt. S.D. Satvalekar, and published by Svādhyāya Maṇḍal, Paradi, Gujarat.

In 1946-47 when I was teaching for a brief while at S.V. College, Tirupati, the college had the privilege of having

Paṇḍitarāja D.T. Tatacharya, a great Mīmāṁsaka and a true Vaiṣṇava, as one of its seniormost and respected teachers. Listening to his extremely rare public speeches and having occasional conversations with him made me somewhat cognizant of the importance of Mīmāṁsā. I came to grasp its great significance only by the late 50s. When I was working in the Andhra University, Professor C. Kunhan Raja joined it in 1954 and was with us for about five or six years. He was by then a famous scholar who had been studying the Veda for about forty years, edited a number of Vedabhāṣyas and translated classics on Vedānta and Mīmāṁsā. While with us he brought out: (1) the *Asyavāmasya Hymn* (1956) with the text and the bhāṣyas of Sāyaṇa and Ātmānanda and his own translation and notes; and (2) *Vedas* (1957) containing his provoking public lectures in the university. I enjoyed the friendship of this eminent scholar who combined traditional learning with a mastery of modern critical methodology, but, above all, thought independently and formulated views, different from those held by most authorities. He declared himself to be a Mīmāṁsaka in whose philosophy God had no place. The many discussions we had stimulated and helped my Vedic studies.

During 1975-78 I was not only the head of the Sri Venkateswara University at Tirupati, but was also for an year or so Chairman of the Kendriya Sanskrit Vidyapeetha located there. This enabled me to meet and have often long and rewarding conversations with Professors E.R. Sreekrishna Sarma and S. Sankaranarayanan of the university, and Professors M.D. Balasubrahmanyam and N.S. Ramanuja Tatacharya of the Vidyapeetha.* While all of them are traditional scholars of the highest order, the first and the third had done excellent work in Vedic studies, the second is proficient in Vedapāṭha, Nyāya, history and epig-

* The first three have retired; the last is Vice-Chancellor of Rashtriya Sanskrit Vidyapitha, Tirupati.

raphy, and the fourth is an adept in three śāstras: Nyāya, Mīmāṃsā and Viśiṣṭādvaita Vedānta. Naturally, I was intellectually much enriched in those three years through my contacts with these paṇḍita-diggajas.[12] When I had a problem with a few Vedic passages, a discussion with Prof. Sankaranarayana solved it; and in a couple of cases when I could not trace a reference or needed one or two more to strengthen an argument, Professor Balasubrahmanyam, in consultation with Professor Tatacharya, provided them.

Professor P. Sriramachandrudu, Emeritus Professor of Sanskrit, Osmania University, one of our eminent savants in both Vedānta and Alaṅkāra-śāstra, who at the same time is well-conversant with modern critical methodology, kindly read the typescript of this work. From 1985 whenever I got a śāstraic doubt I got it cleared by a discussion with him and much of what I wrote in Sanskrit or on Vedānta was first read by him. For this I am very much indebted to him.

I must make it clear that none of the authors or scholars mentioned in the Preface are in any way responsible for the views, interpretations and comments contained in the book, for all of which only I am responsible.

The first chapter of this book is a revised version, with augmented notes, of an article which appeared in the *Triveni*, vol. 46, no. 4, Jan.-March,1978, under the title "Some Thoughts on the Veda and Its Study", based on my address delivered on December 27,1976, in the Veda Śāstra Āgama Vidvat Sadas, in Śrī Veṅkaṭeśvara temple, Tirumala. The matter in the second chapter served as the basis for a lecture on April 10, 1992, in the University of California, Los Angeles, under the auspices of the Southern California Seminar on South Asia, in conjunction with the Interdisciplinary Centre for Study of Religion and the Committee for South and Southeast Asia at UCLA. The last chapter incorporates, besides others some of the points made in my lecture "Advaitic Anticipations in the Veda" delivered on June 25,1988, in Gurukula Kangri Vishwavidyalaya, Haridvar. I am beholden to the organisers of that Sadas, the editor of

Triveni and the authorities of this Vishwavidyalaya, who gave me opportunities to present my ideas at different times.

I have presumed to dignify this work by entitling it "Śrutyarthaparyālocanā" (Deliberation on the import of the Veda). It is a phrase which occurs in Rāmānujācārya's *Vedārthasaṅgraha*, perhaps the shortest, most brilliant and yet comprehensive lecture ever delivered on the meaning of the Veda.[13] In English I have called it simply *Vedic Hermeneutics*,[14] as it just deals with the interpretation of this scripture.

I am grateful to Professor Dr. Mandan Mishra, Vice-Chancellor, Shri Lal Bahadur Shastri Rashtriya Sanskrit Vidyapeetha, New Delhi, for having accepted this work as his university's publication. He is a highly renowned savant in Mīmāṁsā, who has received prestigious awards from the Central and State Governments for the work he has done; and he is the principal disciple of one of the greatest contemporary Mīmāṁsakas, the late Mm. Paṇḍita Pattabhirama Shastri. It is an honour for any scholar to have his book brought out under the auspices of Professor Mishra and his university.

January 1993 K. SATCHIDANANDA MURTY

NOTES

1. A.A: Macdonell, *A Practical Sanskrit Dictionary.*
2. *Ibid.*
3. Upāsanā is steadfastness of mind in the thing meditated upon. "Dhyeyavastuni cittasya sthirīkaraṇaṁ".
4. The divine or worshipful Veda. Veda is from vid jñāne: that by which knowledge is obtained. Śruti is from śru śravaṇe: that by which knowledge is heard. For Sri Aurobindo the Veda is a scripture of divine knowledge, divine worship and divine action. Introducing Ṛgveda, X, 71, Sāyaṇa wrote, "Anena sūktena ṛṣiḥ paramapuruṣārthasādhanaṁ parabrahmajñānaṁ stutavān". (By this hymn the ṛṣi praised Brahman-knowledge, the means by which the Supreme Person may be attained). Sāyaṇa quoted *Bṛhad-devatā* in support of this.
5. "Vedatrayī parānandā tattvārthajñānasaṁyutā", 'Gītāmāhātmya' in *Vārāhapurāṇa.*
6. *Hinduism and Buddhism,* p. 5.
7. My Telugu 'Vyākhyāna' on it was published in 1941.
8. On Sept. 3, 1981, I lectured on the Gītā at the Bhandarkar Oriental Research Institute, Poona; my ICPR National Lectures at Guntur on January 18-19, 1988 were on it; and I read a paper on it on September 19, 1992, at Bologna University, Italy.
9. My Telugu 'Vivaraṇa' on it was published in 1946.
10. My book *Revelation and Reason in Advaita Vedānta* was published in India and the USA in 1959, and reprinted in India in 1974.
11. *Vide* Chapter III "Religious Action" in *The Realm of Between,* Simla, 1973.
12. "Scholar-elephants of the quarters" implies that the profundity of their learning is as great as the might of those mythical elephants which support and guard the world. It's a phrase like "a lion or a bull among men".
13. Sudarśanasūri, its commentator, wrote that the Ācārya delivered this lecture in front of Śrī Veṅkaṭeśvara in Tirumala: "Śrībhāṣyakṛdupanyasto yaḥ Śrīśailapateḥ puraḥ, Vedārthasaṅgrahasyāsya . . . "
14. Hermeneutics="interpretation esp. of Scripture or literary texts". *The Concise Oxford Dictionary,* 8th edn., 1990.

CONTENTS

Introduction ix
Preface xix

CHAPTER I

A Right Approach to Sacred Lore

I. Nature & Contents of the Veda 1-6
II. Importance of Knowing the Meaning of the Veda 7-9
III. Interpretations of the Veda 9-13
IV. Eligibility for Study of the Veda 14-17
Notes 18-20

CHAPTER II

The Content of Sacred Lore

I. Interpretative Methodology 21-27
II. Interpretative Freedom Through Tarka 28-31
III. The Vedic, An Argumentative Faith 31-34
IV. Attitudes to the Veda 34-56
V. Epitome 56-65
Notes 66-72

CHAPTER III

Unity and Essence of the Veda

I. Harmonising the Vedas 73-79
II. The Veda and Empirical Knowledge 79-81
III. Yajña 81-90
IV. The Meaning of the Veda 91-93
Notes 94-97

Index 101-105

CHAPTER ONE

A Right Approach to Sacred Lore

I

Nature and Contents of the Veda

In recent years quite a few people, religious as well as secular persons, interested in the preservation and propagation of the Veda have been talking a good deal about promoting and spreading Vedic studies. So, it is appropriate to give some attention to answer the following questions: What is the Veda? What is its special value and significance? How should it be preserved and disseminated? What is the contemporary relevance of its teachings?

Kātyāyana and others defined the Veda as consisting of Mantras and Brāhmaṇas*.[1] The great Vedic commentator Sāyaṇa** mentioned at least three definitions of the Veda: Veda is a heap of words (śabdarāśi) made up of Mantras

---

* 'Mantras are sacred texts which impart a knowledge of things useful in the performance of rituals. Brāhmaṇas are sacred sentences which enjoin something, while Arthavādas are corroborative statements auxiliary to Brāhmaṇas' (Kṛṣṇa Yajvan, *Mīmāṁsā Paribhāṣā*). This is the usual Pūrva Mīmāṁsā view, not accepted by other Vedic interpreters.

** Sāyaṇa is the only person whose bhāṣya on the entire Veda is now available. But the sheer volume of it and some of its internal inconsistencies make it doubtful whether a single person wrote all of it. A single Vyāsa could not have written all the Purāṇas and Upapurāṇas, nor a single Sāyaṇa the entire Vedabhāṣya. Sāyaṇa was probably the chief of a team of scholars who wrote the Bhāṣyas on the different Saṁhitās and Brāhmaṇas.

and Brāhmaṇas (*Ṛgbhāṣyabhūmikā*). Most of the Mīmāṁsakas, Āpastamba, Śaṅkara in the commentary on the Māṇḍūkya Upaniṣad, and others had found this definition acceptable. But on the ground that Yāska[2] and Pāṇini[3] distinguish between Nigama (Chandas) and Brāhmaṇas, Swami Dayananda Saraswati accepted the Saṁhitās containing Mantras only as the Veda. Sri Aurobindo and T.V. Kapali Sastry also maintained that only the Saṁhitās constitute the Veda. Even Prabhākara, a great teacher of Mīmāṁsā, as well as Sāyaṇa gave no real definition of Mantras. Sāyaṇa, in fact, said that Mantras are those which are called as such by those who are well-informed, while Brāhmaṇas make up that part of the Veda which is not made up of Mantras. Madhusūdana Sarasvatī in his *Prasthānabheda* defined the Veda as consisting of Mantras and Brāhmaṇas. According to him, while Mantras are those which throw light on the things and deities connected with rituals, Brāhmaṇas are of three types: Vidhis (injunctions), Arthavādas (implicatory or explanatory sentences), and those which are neither Vidhis nor Arthavādas. Vedāntic sentences are examples of the last type, because while they form a definite portion of the Veda, they are different from Mantras, Vidhis and Arthavādas. In his commentary on the Ṛgveda, Sāyaṇa mentions another definition of the Veda: That by which the means of obtaining the transcendental goal of man is known.[4] A somewhat variant definition is found in his commentary on the Taittirīya Saṁhitā: The Veda is that which makes known the transcendental means of obtaining the desirable and avoiding the undesirable.[5] For example, it is known empirically that women and sandalwood give pleasure to men. The Veda is not for giving such knowledge. But through empirical means we do not know that eating kalañja (a red onion, or meat of an animal killed by a poisoned arrow) is sinful, and that performance of a Jyotiṣṭoma sacrifice leads to heaven. That which gives such knowledge, he says, is

Veda. Sāyaṇa also quotes a passage which says "Dharma* and Brahman** are known from the Veda alone." In the *Prasthānabheda,* Madhusūdana Sarasvatī accepts this and formulates the definition of the Veda as the truly authoritative and valid sentences which have no author and which propound Dharma and Brahman. This is a position generally acceptable to most Mīmāṁsakas and Vedantins.***

If this position is accepted, it follows that the Veda is concerned only with Dharma and Brahman, i.e., with virtue or righteousness and God or the Absolute. Dharma is not a thing, so it cannot be known through empirical means. It can be known only either through human intuition or through a non-human source of knowledge. Intuitions of men differ, so differing insights apprehend Dharma differently. Thus the intuition of some may inform them that eating beef is sinful, while that of others may inform them that eating pork is sinful. If the good is absolute, ways of achieving it (which may loosely be called virtue or righteousness) cannot be many. There must be only one absolute way of achieving the absolute good, and that cannot be known by intuition. So, only an eternal non-human source of knowledge regarding the good and the way of achieving it can provide an infallible guide for righteous action. Reason, experience and culture cannot do so. The Mīmāṁsā and Vedānta schools posit that the Veda is an eternal and infallible source of such knowledge regarding Dharma. Similarly, since God or the Absolute is supersensuous, He or It

---

* Dharma (righteous action) is that which is taught by the Veda as capable of achieving what is beneficial and desirable; Adharma (unrighteous action) is that which is taught by the Veda as capable of bringing on what is harmful and undesirable. These are the usual Pūrva Mīmāṁsā definitions. (Kṛṣṇa Yajvā, *Mīmāṁsā Paribhāṣā*).

** The Absolute, the Ultimate Reality, or God.

*** However, a Mīmāṁsaka who denies Brahman would amend it as: "which propound what is unknowable otherwise".

is beyond sense experience. Inferentially also He or It cannot be grasped, for any kind of inferential act depends upon a knowledge of the relationship between that which is to be proved and its invariable characteristic (e.g., between fire and smoke). But we do not have any such knowledge in the case of God or Brahman. So, the Vedāntin maintains that the Upaniṣadic portion of the Veda—which is also eternal and infallible—is the one and unique source regarding Brahman. In support he would cite Upaniṣadic passages like, Brahman is the person known through the Upaniṣads.[6] It is of great significance that the Mīmāṁsā and Vedānta schools do not admit that knowledge of empirical facts can be derived from the Veda. This implies that the Veda does not contain history or science. An eternal book can neither deal with temporal evanescent events, nor can a book intended to provide knowledge regarding truths unknowable through sense perception and inference contain empirical facts or scientific generalisations based on them. According to this view, ethics consist of command sentences only, which can neither be proved nor disproved, and knowledge of Brahman is not based upon sense perception or reason. This Mīmāṁsā-Vedāntic position avoids all possible conflict between scripture, on the one hand, and history and science, on the other, and it is in accordance with what some schools of contemporary Western philosophy and theology say regarding ethics and knowledge of God: Ethics is non-empirical, non-science; the knowledge of God can only be revelational.

It follows from the above that if there are any passages in the Veda which appear to deal with history or empirical facts, they do not form its intrinsic parts. Also, if there appear to be passages in it, which clearly contradict experience or what can be generalised from experience, they cannot constitute an essential portion of it. As Śaṅkarācārya said, even a hundred Vedic texts cannot establish that fire is cold or does not give light; for no one can cognize what is opposed to what is seen.[7] All classical Indian philosophers are unanimous on this point. What is known beyond doubt through historical research and what is demonstrated as truth through scientific investigations cannot be contradicted by the Veda.

If we consider what the Veda says regarding its own origin, we find at least three sorts of statements: (1) It is the eternal word heard by sages qualified by tapas (askesis).[8] (2) It was born out of sacrifices.[9] (3) The self-existent God manifested it for the welfare of all.[10] The Veda, etc., are the breath of the Great Being.[11] God manifested it through Agni, Vāyu and Sūrya, and Brahmā.[12]

Yāska in the *Nirukta* explained that the eternal Veda manifested itself in the minds of persons performing tapas. So, they become Ṛṣis, i.e., those who were able to intuit the Mantras.[13] Subsequently, the Mīmāṁsā accepted the view that the eternal Veda was just handed down from generation to generation in an unbroken and beginningless way, whereas the Nyāya maintained that it was God's composition revealed to the first born god, Brahmā, and the primeval sages. The Vedānta agreed with the Mīmāṁsā that it was eternal and had no author in the sense in which books like the Rāmāyaṇa had an author, and that God was its source (yoni). On the other hand, Patañjali stated that sages were responsible for the order of the letters, words and sentences in the Veda, implying, perhaps, that the ideas expressed through them were not created.[14]

Today with our knowledge of the history of language and of the origin and development of the universe and man, we cannot accept any book—whether the Veda or the Quran—either as eternal or as composed by God.* It can

---

* From the standpoint that the source of all knowledge and truth is ultimately God, their divine origin has to be admitted wherever they may be found—whether in a scripture, or in a scientific or historical work. But the present argument is not from that standpoint. From that standpoint even their absence or loss should be attributed to Him! (See *Bhagavadgītā*, XV.15, and Śaṅkara on it.)

only be agreed that there are ideas of perennial value and eternal truths, which have been apprehended by the sages and prophets and which are embodied in different scriptures. Some may argue that these have been revealed by God, and others that they have been discovered by men with spiritual capacity. In any case, a scripture is valuable only insofar as it makes known truths unknowable through an empirical source of knowledge (ajñātajñāpanaṁ śāstram) and which remain uncontradicted by human experience and science.

It follows from the above that no scripture is unique and complete. God could not have revealed the entire truth to anyone or to any race, nor could any man or race have discovered the entire truth. As such no scripture is complete. There are profound truths, for example, in the Bhagavadgītā, Śrīmad Bhāgavata, the Tāntric and other books which are not found in the Veda. No scripture is also unique because whether it is a revelation or a discovery, human intellect is responsible for its formulation and expression in a language. So it is limited by the finiteness of the human mind as well as by the culture and time in which the latter functions. We have to also accept that scriptures do contain history mixed with myth and legends, alongside empirical observations as well as valid generalisations based on them mixed with superstitions and wrong generalisations. But these do not form the core of scriptures. The historical and scientific facts they contain provide useful material for reconstructing political and social history and the history of scientific ideas, and the insights regarding man and nature which may be found in them may serve as valuable hypotheses in scientific investigations. However, it is the ethical intuitions, timeless metaphysical truths and spiritual techniques in them which constitute the core, the essence of scriptures.

II
IMPORTANCE OF KNOWING THE MEANING OF THE VEDA

There are many people who believe that the learning of a sacred scripture by heart and its repetition in the approved orthodox way, even without knowing its meaning, is meritorious. We find such a belief in different cultures, Hindu, Buddhist, Islamic and Christian. The chanting of a single appropriate letter, a word or a group of words in the proper way even without understanding their meanings, combined with a firm faith in the intrinsic efficacy of doing so, may lead to spiritual benefit or even psychological or mundane benefit. But without knowing its meaning *and* without a deep, steadfast and firm faith in the intrinsic power of its chanting, if the Veda is learnt by rote and chanted, what purpose does it serve? It may be delightful to hear it, for there is a melody and music in its chanting done according to tradition. Thus it may produce āhlāda (joy) and a catharsis and may even rouse the sense of the numinous, just as a kīrtana of Tyāgarāja might in the listeners who do not know what it means, when sung in the traditional way by a great musician who himself also may not understand its meaning. Even mere Vedic chanting serves to keep alive an immemorial and glorious tradition. By all means let us encourage and support the learning of the Veda by rote and chanting of it in the proper way by as many people as possible. In addition let us admit that understanding its meaning is at least equally, if not more, important. Nowadays often the Veda is chanted by those who do not know its meaning and heard by many who do not understand it,* and both those who chant and hear lack

* In his time Al-Biruni (11th century A.D.) noted, "the Brahmins were reciting the Veda without understanding it and learnt it from one another". He found that "a few among them learn explanations, and fewer still who master its content and interpretation to the point of being able to hold out in controversy". Since then the situation gradually deteriorated further.

a firm faith that the words so chanted and heard have an intrinsic power in them. Yet both, perhaps, feel something; but is that enough? Sould not this state of affairs be transformed?

The Veda itself insists that understanding of its meaning is necessary for obtaining the full benefit from it. A Ṛgvedic passage says: "He who does not know that higher region of truth, what will he do with hymns? Only those who know attain the highest bliss".[15] Another text says:"He who does not know the meaning hears but does not really hear, sees but does not really see, says but does not really understand what he says. But wisdom reveals itself to those who know as does a well-dressed wife to her husband".[16] The *Śatapatha Brāhmaṇa*[17] clearly says that only by knowledge one can ascend to Heaven. The *Nirukta* has gone sofar as to say that he who having learnt the Veda does not know its meaning is like a pillar which merely carries a burden, because only he who knows the meaning attains the auspicious and the holy, having got rid off all his sins through wisdom.[18] The *Bṛhaddevatā* also says: only he who knows (not merely recites) the hymns knows the gods; the deity does not accept the oblation offered without knowledge.[19] Hence, it is clear that sacrifices performed in a mechanical way and hymns repeated in a parrot-like fashion are not completely efficacious.

Most lovers of the Veda today place exclusive emphasis on getting it by heart and repeating it with the proper svara (accent/tone), without understanding its meaning. This is what many Pāṭhaśālās do. While we must admire and salute the Brahmins who have kept alive the chanting of the Veda with svara from immemorial time up to the present day, and while every possible effort should be made to keep alive this great oral tradition, as I already pleaded, at least equal importance must be given to understanding its meaning. If today the teaching of the Veda *is* not as widely known as the teachings of the Bible, the Quran, the

Bhagavadgītā and some other scriptures are, it is because it has not been disseminated among the general public, though since the time of Swami Dayananda Saraswati some efforts have been made to spread its message among all people. Consequently, this most ancient and great scripture remains for many an inert book. Neither its Western philological translations nor its Indian translations based on the *yājñika* (sacrificial) tradition have succeeded in making a spiritual impact on the modern mind. Significant portions of the Saṁhitās and Brāhmaṇas have to be selected, translated, reinterpreted and made accessible in a way appealing and intelligible to the modern mind. It is good that the Upaniṣads/the Bhagavadgītā, a few Tāntric and Yogic treatises and some other Hindu religious works, through various excellent translations, interpretations and expositions, have become living inspirational scriptures, capable of providing direction to many in the modern world. If the Saṁhitā-Brāhmaṇa portion of the Veda is to fulfil a similar role, neither the mere preservation of its chanting with svara nor just its interpretation, philological or sacrificial, will be enough. A critical study, translation and dissemination of its teaching in a way relevant to the present day must be undertaken to make it a living source of spiritual guidance.

III
Interpretations of the Veda

From ancient times the Veda* has been interpreted in many ways. The following three of them are considered important:

1. The ritualists (Yājñikas) have taken the Veda as mainly a source book which informs how to perform rituals

* In this section the discussion is about the interpretation of the Saṁhitās and Brāhmaṇas. All are unanimous that the Upaniṣads are predominantly metaphysical and mystical.

for obtaining this-worldly and other-worldly good. They have gone to the extent of maintaining that there are no statements of facts (bhūtārthavākyas) in it. From this standpoint the entire Upaniṣadic portion becomes just an arthavāda to the commands enjoining acts of meditation conducive to the production of mundane and heavenly benefits, and the gods mentioned in it become hypothetical, i.e., entities supposed to exist. It may be said that Sāyaṇa's bhāṣya is mostly (not certainly wholly) a ritualistic interpretation as it was primarily meant for the yājnikas. So is Skandasvāmi's.

2. There have also been Vedic interpreters down the ages who accepted the Vedic gods as realities, and rituals as acts of propitiation and worship. This means for different purposes different gods have to be worshipped in different ways and certain gods propitiated so that they may not cause harm. This is the polytheistic interpretation of the Veda. It may be argued that Veṅkaṭa-Mādhava's bhāṣya tends to be an example of this kind of interpretation. Most Western interpretations are also of this kind.

3. The Veda has also been interpreted monotheistically. For example, Yāska in the *Nirukta* (VII.4.8, 9) says that all the gods mentioned in the Veda are the limbs of the one Great Self: Ekasyātmano'nye devāḥ pratyaṅgāni bhavanti. Śaunaka's *Bṛhaddevatā* (I.61-65) agrees with this. There are Aitihāsic and Purāṇic texts which assert that the sum and substance of the Veda is the glorification of the One God. According to this view, the various gods who are hymned in it are but functions of the One God. Every hymn in it can be understood as directly referring to the One God, if the words are understood in the etymological (yaugika) way. Perhaps, the commentary of Madhvācārya on the first forty hymns of the Ṛgveda

is the earliest surviving book which gives a monotheistic interpretation of so many hymns. Later Jayatīrtha wrote a commentary on this, and based on these Rāghavendra composed a monotheistic exposition of these hymns. Ātmānanda had written an excellent ādhyātmika (spiritual) bhāṣya on sūkta 164 of the Ṛgveda, I Maṇḍala. In modern times Swami Dayananda Saraswati revived this tradition through his great commentary on the Ṛgveda. Later Sri Aurobindo interpreted the Vedic hymns in a symbolic and mystical way*. T.V. Kapali Sastry wrote *Ṛgbhāṣyabhūmikā* along the lines of Sri Aurobindo's interpretation. It may be remarked that plausible monotheistic and mystical interpretations are possible in the case of many mantras and of a few Brāhmaṇa passages.

What is important is to recognise that from very early times the Veda has been interpreted in many ways. Certain Ṛgvedic passages point out that its hymns are mystical prayers (*niṇyāṇi=rahasyāni stotrāṇi*), and mystical statements (*niṇyā vacāṁsi*) uttered by sages illumined by noble ideas and prayers.[20] The composer of hymns, man, is a mystery (*niṇyaḥ*); and so are the gods.[21] Symbolic explanations of sacrifices are found in the Brāhmaṇas, Āraṇyakas and *Bhagavadgītā*. The *Mahābhārata* indicates that the Vṛtra legend and sacrificial acts can be understood symbolically.[22] If Vṛtra is tamas, ignorance, Indra's vajra is viveka, discrimination, as Nīlakaṇṭha explained. All this shows there was an awareness of the possibility of understanding Vedic

* Sri Aurobindo thought he 'discovered' a considerable body of profound psychological thought" in the Vedic hymns. (*On Veda*, p. 46.) "The central conception of the Veda", he wrote, "is the conquest of the Truth out of the darkness of Ignorance and by the conquest of the Truth the conquest also of Immortality. (*Op. cit.*, p. 278).

legends and rituals symbolically. So, Sri Aurobindo was not unjustified in searching for the inner, symbolic and secret meaning of the Veda. Whether what he claimed to have discovered is really implicit in it or not, and whether it is the only one, is a matter for discussion.

Only by tortuous interpretations it can be shown that the entire Veda is through and through monotheistic, mystical or spiritual. The view that the Veda is just polytheistic is as untenable as the view that it only consists of magical incantations and descriptions of ritualistic acts to be performed mechanically. As Yāska admitted, Vedic mantras contain both higher and lower (uccāvaca) ideas.[23] Profound and eternal metaphysical and psychological truths and ethical intuitions of unsurpassed and perennial value as well as baseless beliefs and untenable ideas are to be found in it; and while it describes spiritual techniques of the highest order, it also elaborately deals with practices and performances fit only to be undertaken by credulous, insensitive and indiscriminating persons. A Purāṇic text says there are three meanings in all the Vedas (*trayorthāḥ sarvavedeṣu*): (the well-known Agni, Fire, etc., the One God within them and the spiritual).[24] Let us concentrate on the ādhyātmika meaning of the Veda—its spiritual essence. Let competent scholars attempt to discover it in their own ways without depending on others.

From what has been said, it follows that it is wrong to take Yāska, Sāyaṇa, or anyone modern as omniscient and infallible. Yāska was not the first to interpret Vedic words as he did. He referred to a Nighaṇṭu with Samāmnāya which he cited and explained. He had predecessors like Śākapūṇi, Audumbarāyaṇa, Aupamanyava and others. He referred to alternate ways of understanding Vedic words and passages. While his was the Nairuktika (etymological-definitional) tradition, he was aware of other traditions of Vedic interpretation such as the Aitihāsika (historical, e.g., those who take Indra-Vṛtra battles as real incidents) and the Yājñika (sacrificial). Śaunaka's *Bṛhaddevatā* pointed out what it considered as shortcomings or errors in Yāska. Yāska, for example, interpreted the phrase "pañcajanāḥ" as the four varṇas (castes) and the Niṣādas. The *Bṛhaddevatā* informs us that it is possible to understand it in other ways also, e.g. : (1) The five fires, (2) the four chief priests and the yajamāna (sacrificer), and (3) the eye, ear, mind, speech and breath. It says the spiritualists accept the third meaning.[25] Most of the Western as well as contemporary Indian scholars accepted Sāyaṇa's bhāṣya, as it was complete and accessible. For them the Veda appeared to be polytheistic and ritualistic only, or at least mainly so, though, according to Sāyaṇa himself, its purport (tātparya) is not that. They forget that Sāyaṇa himself was a Vedāntin who believed that the Saṁhitā-Brāhmaṇa portion leads up to and culminates in the Upaniṣadic portion of the Veda which taught Advaita. It is possible to argue that the purport of the Saṁhitā-Brāhmaṇa portion is also spiritual, monotheistic and mystical. Let students of Vedabhāṣyas in all Pāṭhaśālās be exposed to bhāṣyas of not only Sāyaṇa, but also of Madhva, Dayananda, Kapali Sastry and others. Let it also be remembered that while the Pūrva aad Uttara Mīmāṁsās claim to systematise, harmonise and interpret the Veda, the Ithihāsas and Purāṇas* claim to amplify and supplement the meaning of the Veda.[26] It is for scholars to decide how far these claims are justified.

---

* Hindu Tradition (i) regards the *Mahābhārata* as the fifth Veda, the *Bhagavadgīta* as the 'nectar milked from the Upaniṣadic cows', (ii) considers that through Vālmīki the Veda actually became the *Rāmāyaṇa* when the Supreme Person knowable by it was born as Daśaratha's son, and (iii) conceives the *Bhāgavata* to be the ripe delicious fruit which dropped from the wish-fulfilling Vedic tree. (i) Sarvopaniṣado gāvaḥ—dugdhaṁ gītāmṛtaṁ mahat. (ii) Vedavedye pare puṁsi jāte Daśarathātmaje, Vedaḥ Prācetasādāsītsākṣādrāmāyaṇātmanā. (iii) Nigamakalpatarorgalitaṁ phalam—Bhāgavataṁ rasālayaṁ. One who has seriously and sincerely studied and pondered over these books for long and grasped the core of their teaching would not scoff at this tradition.

IV
Eligibility for Study of the Veda

One of the great obstacles to the preservation and propagation of the Veda has been denial of universal access to it. For several centuries only the traivarṇika men (men of the three upper castes) have been generally considered eligible to undertake Vedic study, but in effect it has been the exclusive privilege and prerogative of male Brāhmins only. Even today most Brāhmins who have learnt the Veda, either with or without meaning generally do not teach it to women, śūdras and others. But the Veda itself does not say that it is meant for any particular sex, caste or race. On the contrary, it declares that it is meant for all. There is the following Yajurvedic text: "Just as I have revealed this auspicious word to all human beings, so must you. I have revealed the Vedic truth to Brāhmins, Kṣhatriyas, Śūdras, Āryas, personal servants (svāya) and to the lowest of Śūdras (araṇāya) also".[27] There is also the following Atharvavedic text: "O Man, I, being of the nature of truth and being unfathomable, have revealed the true Vedic knowledge; so I am he who gave birth to the Veda. I cannot be partial either to a Dāsa (slave) or an Ārya; I save all those who behave like myself (i.e., impartially) and follow my truthful commands".[28] The Veda is a universal scripture.

We find examples of Śūdras and sons of slaves propagating Vedic hymns. Some examples may be given: Kavaṣa Ailuṣa propagated Sūktas 30 to 34 of the Ṛgveda, Maṇḍala, X, Anuvāka III. This is known from the *Aitareya* and *Kauṣītakī Brāhmaṇas,* the *Ṛgveda Anukramaṇikā,* and Sāyaṇa's bhāṣya. Kakṣīvān propagated Sūktas 116 to 126 of the Ṛgveda, Maṇḍala I, Anuvāka XVII. While his mother was a female slave of the king of Aṅgadeśa, his father Dīrghatamas, was the son of a woman who, while *enceinte* with him, had an incomplete, though willing, sexual union with her husband's brother. That slave woman and

Dīrghatamas were not a married couple, theirs was a momentary coming together, adventitious and loveless.[29] Yet, both the father, Dīrghatamas, and the son, Kakṣīvān, became great Ṛṣis, with many Sūktas to their credit. This is known from Kātyāyana's *Sarvānukramaṇī*, the *Bṛhaddevatā* (IV.11 f.) and Sāyaṇa's bhāṣya (I. 125.1, 141-3 & 158-4). Mahīdāsa Aitareya was a slave or a Śūdra by birth. He was the son of a Brāhmin sage and a lowcaste woman, Itarā. He became a great sage, who propagated the Aitareya Brāhmaṇa and Āraṇyaka. (Sāyaṇa, Introductory bhāṣya on Aitareya Brāhmaṇa.) According to the *Chāndogya Upaniṣad,* Aitareya by knowing that "verily, a person is a sacrifice" (puruṣo vāva yajñaḥ) and by praying to gods at critical times, lived in full health for 116 years. Critical study also shows that Janaśruti was a Śūdra, and Satyakāma Jābāli was the son of a servant woman who lived with many men. According to the Upaniṣads; both received the highest Vedāntic teaching. Raikva, the former's teacher, did not certainly belong to the three upper castes, but knew the highest truth. According to internal evidence, women were also eligible for Vedic study. The 179th Sūkta of the Ṛgveda, Maṇḍala I, Anuvāka XXIII, was propagated by Lopāmudrā, a woman; while the 91st Sūkta of the Ṛgveda, Maṇḍala VIII, Anuvāka I, was propagated by Apalā, another woman. The *Ṛgveda Anukramaṇikā* and Sāyaṇa's bhāṣya inform us to this effect. It is well-known that ladies Gārgī and Maitreyī were great sages who knew the highest Upaniṣadic truths (*Bṛhadāraṇyaka Upaniṣad*). Patañjali's *Mahābhāṣya* informs us that a Brāhmin woman studied the Mīmāṁsā developed by Kāśakṛtsna. This means she studied the Veda also.

Nowhere in the Saṁhitā-Brāhmaṇas or the Upaniṣadic portions is any caste, sex or race excluded from studying and benefiting from the Veda. The sentence "Women and Sūdras should not be taught the Veda" (*na strī śūdro vedam adhīyātām*), frequently cited by those who advocate prohibition of access to the Veda to lower castes and women, is not a Vedic text. Nor is the citation 'The Veda should not be studied by the Śūdra' (*Śūdreṇa nādhyetavyaṁ*) in the Pūrva Mūmāṁsā Sūtra/Bhāṣya (VI.1. 37-8) found anywhere in the Veda.* However, there are passages in some Smṛtis which lay down such a prohibition. On the contrary, there are passages in other smṛtis and kalpa which maintain that Śūdras can receive Upanayana and study the Veda.[30] There is considerable evidence that Śūdras of good families, endowed with good qualities, were taught all the śāstras, except the Saṁhitās, without Upanayana.[31] The Vedānta Sūtras, I.3.34-38, have been interpreted by almost all the medieval bhāṣyakāras as prohibiting Śūdras from Vedic study. Of them Śaṅkara is the most liberal, for he at least admits that some Śūdras may, like Vidura and Dharmavyādha, attain Brahman-knowledge due to the results of their actions in past lives, and that all the four castes are free to attain Brahman-knowledge through Itihāsa-purāṇas. Ārya Samājist scholars, however, interpreted the relevant Vedānta Sūtras as permiting Śūdras also access to Vedic study.

While there is no Vedic text which prohibits Śūdras from studying the Veda, there is a Taittirīya text which says they are not eligible to perform sacrifices. "*Tasmāt śūdro yajñe anavaklaptaḥ*".[32] Commenting on Pāṇini's sūtra which mentions Anirvasita Śūdras, Patañjali explains that not all Śūdras are prohibited from performing sacrifices. Some are (Niravasita Śūdras) and some are not (Aniravasita).[33] Commenting on this, Kaiyaṭa says that Śūdras are eligible to perform the five Mahāyajñas (great sacrifices).[34] These include the Brahmayajña, which means Vedic study (Svādhyāya), Sandhyāvandana, Japa, etc. So, as Nāgeśa clarified (*Uddyota*), this Taittirīya text prohibits Śūdras from performing only sacrifices like Agnihotra and not the five great sacrifices. This makes them eligible for Vedic study.

* No one who has cited these two has found for them any loci in the śruti.

The Mīmāṁsā Śūtras, VI. 1. 24 to 38, have been interpreted by their medieval commentators as prohibiting Śūdras from Vedic study and sacrifices. The Ārya Samājists, however, do not accept such an interpretation and maintain that according to Jaimini, all are eligible to study the Veda and perform Vedic rituals, because their reward is desired by all and whoever has the capacity to undertake and complete them can do so.[35] Even the medieval commentators admit that Bādari, a great sage, who is cited by Jaimini, maintained that all, including Śūdras, are eligible to perform Vedic sacrifices. Similarly, sages like Aitiśāyana denied the eligibility of women to Vedic study and perform sacrifices, while Bādarāyaṇa and Jaimini asserted to the contrary. Some smṛtis make scriptural study mandatory to women.[36]

To summarise, the Veda itself claims to be an universal scripture meant for all human beings. Whoever has the sincere desire (arthitva) and capacity (sāmarthya) is eligible to study it either in the original or in its translations. Some smṛtis and sages assert that Śūdras and women are not entitled to Vedic study, while other smṛtis and sages maintain that they too are entitled. Good sense, justice and reason demand that the latter view be accepted. Everyone has the right to the highest wisdom from the best source available. Moreover, as the Western scholars (who according to some smṛti writers would be mlecchas) as well as those who are not traivarṇikas (e.g., Prince Dara Shikoh, Swami Vivekananda and Sri Aurobindo) have studied, edited, translated, expounded, or published the Vedas and Upaniṣads, it is not only unjust but ridiculous to support any more the tabu on Vedic study. People of all castes including the 'Harijans' and 'Girijans' and of all nationalities—irrespective of their sex—should be encouraged to study the Veda

kṛṇvanto viśvamāryam

(making the entire world Āryan, i.e., noble and enlightened.)

NOTES

1. "Mantrabrāhmaṇayorvedanāmadheyam", *Kātyāyanapariśiṣṭapratijñāsūtra,* 1.1. *Āpastambaśrautasūtra,* 24.1.31."Mantrabrāhmaṇaṁ veda ityācakṣate", *Bodhāyanagṛhyasūtra,* 2.6.2. "Mantrāśca brāhmaṇañca vedaḥ", Śabara's bhāṣya, 2.1.33.
2. *Nirukta,* V. 3.4: "Ityapi nigamo bhavati, iti brāhmaṇam".
3. IV. 2.66.
4. Bhāṣya on Ṛgveda.
5. "Iṣṭaprāpti-aniṣṭaparihārayor alaukika upāyaḥ vedaḥ".
6. "Taṁtvaupaniṣadaṁ puruṣaṁ pṛcchāmi".
7. *Gītābhāṣya,* 18.67. *Bṛhadāraṇyakabhāṣya,* 1.4.10.
8. "Vācā virūpa nityayā", *Ṛgveda,* VIII, 75-6.
9. "Yajñat ṛcaḥ sāmāni jajñire", *Ṛgveda,* X.90-9.
10. "Yasmāddṛuco apātakṣan...", *Atharva Veda,* X.7.70. "Svayambhūr yāthātathyato arthān vyadadhāt...", *Yajurveda,* 40-8.
11. "Asya mahato bhūtasya niḥśvasitaṁ", *Bṛhadāraṇyaka Upaniṣad,* II.4.10.
12. "Yo vai vedāṁśca prahiṇoti...", *Śvetāśvatara Upaniṣad,* VI. "Agne Ṛgvedo ... ", *Śatapatha Brāhmaṇa,* XI. 4.2.3.
13. *Nirukta,* I.20; II. 11.
14. *Mahābhāṣya* on Sūtra, IV. 3. 101.
15. "Yastanna veda kiṁṛcā kariṣyati? Ya itta dvidusta ime samāsate", *Ṛgveda,* I.164.39.
16. "Uta tvaḥ paśyanna dadarśa...jāyeva patya uśatī suvāsāḥ", *Ṛgveda,* X. 71.4.
17. X. 5.4.
18. "Sthāṇurayam bhārahāraḥ ... ", cited in *Nirukta,* I. 18.
19. "Yā ṛco ha yo veda sa veda devān". "Avijñānapradiṣṭam hi havirneheta daivatam". —*Bṛahaddevatā,* VII. 130, 132.
20. "Amūrā viśvā ... na vām niṇyanyacite abhūvan". *Ṛgveda,* VII. 61.5. "Etā viśvā viduṣe tubhyam ... niṇyā vacāṁsi." *Ṛgveda,* IV. 3.16.
21. "Na vijānāmi yadivedamasmi niṇyaḥ saṁnaddho manasā carāmi". *Ṛgveda,* I. 164.37.
22. *Mahābhārata,* XIV. 11.7-20.
23. "Uccāvacaiḥ abhiprāyaiḥ ṛṣīṇām mantradṛṣṭayo bhavanti". *Nirukta,* VII. 2.
24. "Ṛgarthaśca trividho bhavati ekastāvatprasiddhāgnyādirūpaḥ aparastadantargateśvaralakṣaṇaḥ anyo'dhyātmarūpaḥ." Jayatīrtha, *Rgbhāṣyaṭīkā.*
25. VII. 67. 71: "cakṣuḥ śrotram mano vāk ca prāṇaśceti ātmavādinaḥ".
26. "Itihāsapurāṇābhyāṁ vedaṁ samupabṛṁhayet". *Mahābhārata,* I.

1. 267. It occurs in *Nāradīya Purāṇa* also.

27. "Yathemāṁ vācaṁ kalyāṇīṁ ... brahmarājanyābhyāṁ śūdrāya cāryāya ca svāya cāraṇāya ca". *Śukla Yajurvedasaṁhitā*, 26.2.

28. "Satyamahaṁ gabhīraḥ ... na me dāso nāryo mahitvā vrataṁ mīmāya yadahaṁ dhariṣye. *Atharva Vedasaṁhitā*, 5.11.3. Quoting śruti texts which make niṣādas eligible for yajñas, slaves (dāsas) eligible for the hearing and study of Vedic sentences, barbers and carvers of slaughtered sacrificial animals (śamitṛ) eligible for hearing of certain Vedic mantras, and married women as well as virgins eligible for Vedic recitation (vācana) and murmured prayer (japa), Ātmānanda raises the pūrvapakṣa (objection): "Like that śūdras also have a right to have Brahman-knowledge direct from the śruti". "Tathaiva brahmavidyāyāṁ śrauta evādhikāro bhaviṣyati śūdrasyāpi". He dismisses the objection by saying that cannot be so, because prohibition of such a right is stronger and śūdras' right is opposed to many śrutis and smṛtis. "maivam niṣedhasya balīyatvāt anekaśrutivirodhācca". But he, like others, did not quote a single negative śruti sentence which can be located anywhere in the Veda as now available. He is just content to conclude: "It does not matter if there is no such right, as śūdras have the right to know and appropriate the import of śruti without its study". "Mā bhūcchūdrasya śrautapūrvo'dhikāraḥ ... śrutipāṭhābhāve'pi śrutyarthāvadhāraṇapakṣo'styeva". (Ātmānanda, *op. cit.*)

29. For details, see C. Kunhan Raja, *Asyavāmasya Hymn*, Madras, 1956, pp. xxi-xxii; *The Vedas*, Waltair, 1957, pp. 126-28. Ātmānanda claimed to be a descendant of Dīrghatamas. See the latter's life sketch at the end of Ātmānanda's bhāṣya in Kunhan Raja's first book.

30. (1) "Śūdrāṇām aduṣṭakarmaṇām upanayanam". *Pāraskara Gṛhya Sūtra*, 2.6 Āpastamba prohibited upanayana for Brahmins with bad qualities.

(2) "Śūdrāṇāṁ brahmacaryatvaṁ munibhiḥ kaiścidiṣyate". *Yogī Yājñavalkya*, ch. 2.

(3) "Atra ca śūdrā Vājasaneyinaḥ iti Vasiṣṭhavākyāt". *Saṁskāra Mayūkha*, pa. 85.

(4) "Śūdro vā caritavrataḥ". *Vṛddha Gautama Smṛti*, ch. 16.

(5) *Nṛsiṁhamantrarājakalpa*, quoted by Ātmānanda on *Ṛgveda*, I. 164.16, asserts eligibility of Śūdras and women for Brahman-knowledge direct from śruti sentences.

(6) A *Mahābhārata* śloka, cited by Ātmānanda (*ibid.*) enjoins that a Brahman-knower ought not to be indifferent to whosoever seeks Brahman-knowledge, as it is his duty to enlighten a seeker in some way or other, through Vedic, Purāṇic or worldly (laukika) words, according to what the latter is entitled to.

31. "Śūdramapi kulaguṇasampannaṁ mantravarjam anupanītam adhyāpayedityete". *Suśruta,* Sūtrasthāna.
32. *Taittirīya Saṁhitā,* VII, 1.1.6.
33. *Mahābhāṣya* on *Sūtra,* II. 4.10.
34. "Śūdrāṇām pañcamahāyajñānuṣṭhāne adhikāro'stīti bhāvaḥ". Kaiyaṭa.
35. *Mīmāṁsā Sūtra,* VI. 1. 4-5. These sūtras are: "Because the reward of an action is desired, *all* are entitled to perform it". "Or, the command by reason of its connection with the Veda, applies to a doer who can complete the whole".
36. "Yacca āmnāyo vidadhyāt". *Gobhila Gṛhya Sūtra,* I. 2.

CHAPTER TWO

The Content of Sacred Lore

I
Interpretative Methodology

An ancient work venerated as a sacred book, held to contain words of power, the whole of which or even portions of which, read or recited is believed to confer material and/or spiritual benefit, and, moreover, the meaning of which understood and assimilated is also accepted as providing liberating knowledge, can be approached in a variety of ways by scholars. They can determine its age, meaning, compositeness or otherwise and other matters by the techniques of grammatical and logical analysis, invoking the help of advanced historical and comparative linguistics and philology, and after a study of (a) different commentaries and explanations of it composed at different times, and of (b) references to it in religious and secular literatures, inscriptions, etc., and (c) by other scientific methods. No single scholar or a group of scholars working at a time or cumulatively at different times in this way can, perhaps, ever reach unanimous, objective and final conclusions on all matters relating to such a work, and even if they do they may not be convincing either to the impartial or to the faithful; and the members of each of these groups may not have identical views on them.[1] What is taken to be the Veda by, e.g., Yāska and Śaunaka, Pāṇini and Patañjali, the Itihāsas and Pūrāṇas, Jaimini and Bādarāyaṇa, Śaṅkara, Rāmānuja and Madhva, Skandasvāmi and Sāyaṇa, is *the* Veda or *the* śruti which has influenced millions for centuries, giving them directly or through later works dependent on them knowledge: by which (a) they can mould their lives and (b) attain the ultimate good. For comprehending its spiritual significance, the Veda has to be taken as a whole, its meaning and tātparya (purport) apprehended according to interpretative principles formulated from immemorial times, *IF* its empathic understanding is the goal. Such an understanding need not necessarily end in accepting as truth what is so understood.

A summary of the interpretative method acceptable to Advaita Vedānta (which is in broad agreement with that of Bhāṭṭa Mīmāṁsā school) will now be presented, following what I earlier wrote.[2] The fundamental or basic meaning (mukhya artha) of a sentence, passage, chapter or an entire book is what may be called its purport (tātparya). In a sentence the meanings of words are the content of words *through* themselves, and the meaning of the sentence, as a whole, is the content of words through purport. When two or more sentences form a unitary passage, several sentences a chapter, and a number of chapters a book, while each sentence has its own meaning *through* itself, by rightly correlating sentences the purport of the passage, then by rightly correlating the passages of a chapter the purport of the chapter, and through correlation of the chapters the purport of the book as a whole may be obtained. Purport is the meaning of words leading to valid knowledge, and is the property of words. The purport of a sentence may be an activity or a fact. The literal or direct meaning of a sentence may be an activity or a fact. The literal or direct meaning of a sentence may not be its purport; in which case its implied meaning would be its purport. In cases in which to grasp the true purport of a sentence its implied meaning has to be depended upon, as the latter is not something which is not at all expressed by the sentence, and as the direct significance of the words is not *entirely* abandoned, the implied meaning is itself the basic meaning.

A śāstra (sacred book) is a vast array of sentences, and unless a coherent co-ordination of them is achieved, one cannot develop a perspective regarding its teaching. Selective judgement has to be exercised to achieve this by picking out some sentences, or groups of them, which are significant from out of countless others. The selection has to be based on a conception of the *importance* of their meaning.[3] Sentences or groups of them have to be juxtaposed and correlated, and from out of them the recurrent theme[4] has to be discovered; and with reference to it a coherent order has to be introduced into the welter of scriptural sentences. Irrelevant sentences (i.e., those which have nothing to do with the real aims of human life, puruṣārtha) have to be ignored; useless sentences (those which merely give empirical information) have to be passed by, for a śāstra is for informing that which cannot be known otherwise;[5] apparent meanings have to be rejected; and the inner core of truth has to be grasped. All this can be done only if the recurrent dominant theme, in other words *purport*, is discovered; for once this is done, in terms of it all scriptural statements can be rightly interrelated[6] and a consistent doctrine developed out of them. *Purport*, therefore, provides the clue to scriptural understanding.[7]

As a result of some hundreds of years of discussion, in the 16th century Dharmarāja formulated a definition of tātparya as follows: "It is the capacity of words to produce a clear conception or understanding (pratīti) of something, there being no articulation with an intention to produce another conception or understanding."[8] Knowledge of the tātparya of a sentence is an essential condition for the knowledge of its meaning.

For determining the purport of a scripture six criteria[9] have been set forth: unity of the initial and concluding passages, the recurrence of theme, the new conclusion sought to be brought out, the fruitfulness of such a conclusion, the commendation or criticism of it throughout, and the argument throughout. Among them the first one is the most important. But if in trying to harmonize the initial and concluding passages, it is found that there is an opposition between the two, the subsequent is to be interpreted in conformity to the earlier; and if that too is not possible, i.e., if both appear not to form a single topic,[10] then the subsequent should be regarded as an altogether new one. This is the principle of the 'domination of the initial passage'.[11] On the other hand, if what is said later contradicts what is said earlier, and if its sense is not intelligible unless what is said earlier is sublated, then this should be done.[12] This, of course, does not mean that every following cognition or statement should be taken to disprove the antecedent one. A false cognition may follow a right one, but sooner or later a false cognition is bound to be sublated by a right one, while the right one endures. Similarly, if even in an authoritative book sometimes a right view is stated first to rebut a wrong view stated later, it should be understood that the statement of the erroneous view is meant to precede that of the right one; for then only there will be meaningful sequence.[13]

While the six criteria and the two principles, etc., mentioned above may help in scriptural interpretation, as selective judgement based on one's idea of importance is unavoidable in interpretation, all such interpretation is more or less subjective. It has been authoritatively pointed out that even in the scientific mode of thought, careful continuous observation of facts, concentrated attention to what is relevant and upholding of a doctrine, presuppose and are sustained by a notion or sense of importance.[14] The great masters of Mīmāṁsā and Vedānta (e.g., Kumārila and Prabhākara, Śaṅkara and Rāmānuja) knew and applied these criteria and principles, and yet arrived at different interpretations. Among such, can it be said that one was right and others were wrong, or all of them wrong, for to judge so should not one possess intellect, learning and spiritual achievement superior to theirs? Does it not also follow that, for instance, Mm. A. Chinnaswami Sastri's interpretation of a Vedic sūkta may not be less valid or more subjective than that of A.B. Keith?

Bhāṣyas on the Veda do not seem to contain theoretical discussions of principles of scriptural interpretation. However, Ram Gopal in his excellent scholarly monograph[15] on this subject has quoted brief comments relating to these from two of them. Veṅkaṭa-Mādhava (9th or 10th century) of Coladeśa, whose brief and complete bhāṣya on the Ṛgveda is available, has remarked: "The wise determine the meanings of mantras with the help of other mantras of clear import contained in the other śākhās".[16] Uvaṭa (first half of 11th century) of Ujjayinī in his commentary on Śukla Yajurveda observed that śruti shows that a sound knowledge of words through etymology is the cause of prosperity.[17]

Most of the Western Indologists translating or writing on the Veda on the whole relied excessively on comparative philology and comparative mythology, and consciously or unconsciously approached it as a hoary collection of hymns of a primitive people, preserved for thousands of years by an oral tradition. They were busy dating it through an analysis of its language and ideas, assigning different portions of it to different periods, and gathering historical and anthropological facts about the authors of its hymns and their society. The majority of them did not seek to study and understand the Veda in the way in which for thousands of years those who believed it to be a holy book did. If one desires to understand the spiritual significance of the Bible, one ought to approach it in the way persons like St. Augustine, St. Thomas Aquinas or Martin Luther did, and for the Quran it should be in the way of those like al-Ghazali. The Western scholars had access only to Sāyaṇa's bhāṣya and as it was mainly intended to help those who wanted to understand and perform rituals, the impression they got of Vedic religion was of a predominantly polytheistic, priestly, mechanical and sacrificial religion. At a certain stage in the course of Vedic studies, the principle of Roth that Sāyaṇa must not be read if one were to understand the Veda became the guiding principle. One is reminded in this connection of a verse by a Sanskrit poet Murāri: "The monkey-soldiers of Rāma only crossed the ocean. But its depth is known only to mount Mandara, whose huge body in order to churn the ocean with it was immersed into the ocean down to the netherworld beneath it."[18] The depths of any sacred lore can be plumbed only by the discerning scholars who deeply dive into it with the aid provided by those who have already done so and garnered some of the precious things underneath.

There is a story that Rāmānujācārya attentively read the Rāmāyaṇa one hundred and eight times before he could understand it well. Probably this is one of the best ways for comprehending any great and profound work. It is interesting to note that Abel Bergaigne commended something like this in the case of the Veda: "Without neglecting the light which might be shed by other sources, the best method of understanding the Ṛgveda would be to read it incessantly, not hymn by hymn, but verse by verse, and in a manner even word by word."[19] According to the Taittirīya Upaniṣad, after having taught the Veda the teacher should exhort the departing students: "Speak the truth. Practise virtue. Neglect not study of the Veda." Svādhyāyān mā pramadaḥ.[20] The Upaniṣad enjoins that Vedic study ought to be continued throughout life even as speaking of truth and practice of virtue, and in an earlier passage equates it with the right, the true, *tapas*, etc.

This section may be concluded by referring to what three of the best and sympathetic Western Vedists have written on understanding the Veda. Whitney, translator of the Atharva Veda, wrote an article which appeared in the "American Journal of Philology", VII. 2-4, 1886. In it he dealt with the purpose, limitations and method of translating the Upaniṣads, but what he wrote in it is applicable in connection with any portion of the Veda. He mentioned three possible alternatives: (1) to put oneself "frankly and fully under the guidance of a native interpreter"; (2) to give "a conspectus of all native interpretations",——"approving and condemning all with what appeared to be the simple meaning of the text itself"; and (3) "to approach the text only as a philologist bent upon making a version of it exactly as it stands",——"to reproduce the scripture itself in Western guise, as nearly as the nature of the case admits." One who adopts the last, Whitney remarked, "need not be versed in the subtleties of the later Hindu philosophical systems" and need not also "pretend to penetrate to the hidden sense" of everything in the text.[21] Whitney's observations are sober and judicious, and he himself very ably followed the third way.

Three volumes of *Vedische Studien* by Karl Geldner and Richard Pischel appeared from 1889 to 1901. They advocated that the Ṛgveda must be taken in its historical context with its later literature, conceding indigenous tradition a certain significance. According to them, only he can interpret the Ṛgveda who has become, through his study of all spheres of Indian life and literature, familiar with Indian thinking and feeling and can put the Ṛgveda "into organic relation with the general development of Indian people and their spiritual life". Thus Vedic exegesis requires a profound knowledge of the later period and of the Indian commentaries on it; the Ṛgveda should not be explained on the basis of linguistic method alone and should not be considered a prehistoric Aryan work. Holding it to be a "purely Indian work, the most important and ancient product of the Indian spirit", they contended it could be properly understood and interpreted only by scholars well acquainted with all that is Indian.[22] It would be difficult for anyone impartial to disagree with these two scholars in this matter.

II
Interpretative Freedom Through *Tarka*

There is a very striking passage in the *Nirukta* which may be taken as a charter of interpretative freedom. Its background is as follows: As indicated in the earlier chapter, those who had a sākṣātkāra of dharma became ṛṣis (sages); and through personal instruction (upadeśa) they gave mantras to others younger than themselves, who did not have a sākṣātkāra of dharma.[23] Sākṣātkāra, according to a dictionary, is "perception, realisation".[24] The *Nyāya-bhāṣya* defines it as attainment of an object.*[25] The *Bṛhaddevatā* clarified that for a non-ṛṣi there cannot be perception of a mantra.[26] Quoting a *Taittirīya Āraṇyaka* (II.9.) passage, the *Nirukta* at another place said that "to these performing tapas the self-manifesting Veda vouchsafed itself, and that made these ṛṣis. That is known as the ṛṣitva (sageness) of ṛṣis (sages)".[27]

The following poem of a Czech poet, Jan Skacel, seems to express a somewhat analogous idea:

"Poets don't invent poems
The poem is somewhere behind
It's been there for a long time
The poet merely discovers it".

After giving an etymology of the word "akṣara", the *Nirukta* continues: "A similar *abhyūha* arising from reflection on the meaning of mantras may be *abhyūḍha* simultaneously from śruti and tarka (reasoning). *Abhyūha* is an intelligent guess which has a basis, and here the basis is the reflection of the sort mentioned. In fact, Macdonell's dictionary gives "inference" as its equivalent. *Abhyūḍha* is 'drawn

* The *Nyāya-bhāṣya* avers sākṣātkāra may occur to an ordinary man, a sage or God. (It was, of course, not speaking of mantras.) One who has it and with a desire to communicate exactly what he perceived and does so, is a reliable person (āpta). Whether a sage, an Āryan or a Mleccha, it states, whoever does so is an āpta.

out', 'deduced'. The first thing to be noticed is śruti and tarka are here put on the same level. After that the *Nirukta* proceeds to state that mantras should not be interpreted separately, but only contextually.[28] This is important because it is usually thought otherwise by many followers of Nirukta and Mīmāṁsā. Finally comes the striking passage, which is as follows: "When the ṛṣis were flying up*, human beings asked gods, 'who among us will now become a ṛsi?' The gods gifted this *tarka*-ṛṣi to men.** The *tarka* so given was that which was drawn out by inference from reflection on the meaning of mantras. Therefore, whatever a learned man infers (arrives through abhyūha) becomes sageness (ārṣam)***." This is an important text which permits a man versed in the Veda to ponder over its meaning and deduce from it something new, and that will be as good as what a ṛṣi said. In yore there were sages to guide men; now in their place reason shall do so. This is what the gods ordained.

Durgācārya, who perhaps came after Skandasvāmi and Uvaṭa, but preceded Sāyaṇa, who sometimes followed and quoted him, clarified this further. After mentioning that mantras could be interpreted ritualistically (ādhiyājñika), as lauds to gods who are in truth aspects of the One (ādhidaivika), or spiritually (ādhyātmika), he writes: "Therefore from these mantras as many meanings as possible, all of them indeed, may be derived; there is nothing wrong in this".[30] It is extraordinary that unlike the followers of almost all other scriptures and some other Vedic interpreters, these people declared, "our scripture has many meanings, i.e., many in-

---

* It means, when leaving their mortal bodies they were ascending to heaven.

** It means, they presented tarka as ṛṣi, i.e., they gave men reasoning to take the place of a sage. Henceforth, it would guide men as did sages earlier.

*** Ārṣam is what belongs to, is produced by, or is related to a ṛṣi ('Sageness' is accepted by COD.) 'Sagacious' is also quite a good equivalent to ārṣam. Cp. "The cultivated diligent (abhiyuktas) can very well understand the mantras". Kumārila, *Tantravārttika*, I.2.49 end.

terpretations of it are possible. Let all of them be brought forth and used by different people". And the qualified and the competent, they said, were free to interpret in original ways; and such interpretations would be as good as those of ancient sages.

In Śaṅkarācārya's bhāṣya on the Bṛhadāraṇyaka Upaniṣad, occurs the following remarkable interpretation. It is in connection with the explanation of the text, "Meditate on Speech as a cow. . . . Her calf is mind."[31] The bhāṣya on it runs thus: "The word 'Speech' means the Vedas. . . . It is mind (the calf) which makes (stimulates) the Veda (the cow) to reveal its meaning (yield its milk), for the Vedas proceed forward only in a subject thought of by the mind".[32] Unless its calf approaches a milch-cow, takes its teats into its mouth one after another, sucks, and gently butts its mother's udder with its head now and then, milk does not flow into its mouth. Similarly, only a mind which has become active and thought deeply and long about a relevant matter (e.g., Duty and/or the Real), can study the Veda and absorb and digest its meaning. To the unprepared inactive mind the Veda would mean nothing, just as a cow cannot give its milk to its calf which does not approach it and become active in the right manner.

Not only the Upaniṣads, the Saṁhitās too express the same view.[33] While explaining one such passage, quoting from another śākhā a couple of sentences in support, Yāska asserts that any Vedic sentence heard from a teacher and uttered again and again as just recitation without a knowledge of its meaning does not enlighten one. As the 'Vedaness' of the Veda lies in its making known the transcendental means of the supreme human ends, by its repeated meaningless recitation its essential "Vedaness" itself would not be realised. One cannot properly understand the Veda by knowing only words, meanings and grammar. The right knowledge which can throw light on the meaning of the Veda will be achieved only by one who through grammar, etc., probes into the meanings of words and through Mīmāṁsā into its purport.[34] This necessarily leads to a consideration of what Mīmāṁsā is.

III

The Vedic, an Argumentative Faith

From all that has been said in the previous section, the importance of Mīmāṁsā in ascertaining the meaning of the Veda becomes obvious. Now, what is Mīmāṁsā? It is, as S.N. Dasgupta, the best historian of Indian philosophical ideas, said, "rational enquiry" which "attempts at rational conclusions".[35] It is what Kumārila called "a conglomeration of arguments*" (yuktikalāpa), very closely connected to the Veda. According to an old tradition, the Veda itself consists of *tarka***, reasoning, in addition to mantras and brāhmaṇas.[36] According to some, tarka here means Mīmāṁsā. Kumārila mentioned this tradition and justified it by remarking that as Mīmāṁsā is the final summary of the entire Vedic reasoning,[37] it might be called Veda, though it is not really similar to mantras and brāhmaṇas. In some Nyāya works (e.g., of Vācaspati) as well as Mīmāṁsā works (e.g., of Śālikanātha), the inseparability of the Veda and Mīmāṁsā is mentioned. In fact, Vācaspati quotes a verse which says that the *tarka* called Mīmāṁsā, springs from the Veda as a whole.[38] In the bhāṣya on the *Māṇḍūkyakārikā*, Śaṅkarācārya pointed out that the argumentation for showing the non-existence of duality was known from the Upaniṣads.[39] Both Śaṅkara and Sureśvara found "anvaya-vyatireka tarka", i.e., reasoning based upon the presence and absence of connection, as well as analogical reasoning in the Upaniṣads, and gave instances of them. Mere śravaṇa, hearing, of Vedāntic sentences would not produce Brahman-knowledge, unless followed by manana,

---

* *Yukti* is an argument which shows something is probable. See source mentioned in note 2, pp. 142-43, 160, 163.

** According to Nyāya, *tarka* is a conjecture, a hypothesis for the sake of obtaining certain knowledge of something. 'Tattvajñānārthamūhastarkaḥ'.

which is meditation through reasoning, and nididhyāsana, contemplation. According to Śaṅkara, the oneness of the Self is clearly shown only when scriptural testimony together with tarka demonstrate it; the meaning of scriptural texts should be explained and tested in the light of arguments.[40] Vācaspati asserted Vedānta-Mīmāṁsā is indeed *tarka*, aided by other *tarkas* found in Mīmāṁsā and Nyāya.[41] So, in Vedānta tarka is needed (i) to ascertain the purport of scriptural passages, (ii) to remove doubts (saṁśaya) and contrary beliefs (viparyāsa), and (iii) to convince us of the probability of the existence of what is to be known, i.e., Brahman (prameya sambhava niścaya).[42] The *tarka* or reasoning needed by Vedānta must be (i) dependent on scripture; (ii) must elucidate the content of scripture, and (iii) must not be opposed to it.[43] Madhusūdana Sarasvatī maintained that Vedānta vicāra (pondering over Upaniṣad vākyas) is nothing but śravaṇa, aided by manana and nididhyāsana; and that such śravaṇa is of the nature of anvaya-vyatireka tarka.[44]

Both Mīmāṁsā and Vedānta are hermeneutic philosophies, in which exegesis, apologetics, epistemology, metaphysics and ethics are synthesised. Mīmāṁsā is primarily concerned with duty and/or righteousness and Vedānta with the knowledge of ultimate reality. Only from the Veda are dharma and Brahman to be known;[45] as they cannot be known from any other source the Veda has them as its objects.[46] According to both Gauḍapāda and Śaṅkara, the meaning of śruti can be only that which is ascertained to be true and in accordance with methodical reasoning, and nothing else. Niścitaṁ yuktiyuktaṁ ca yattadbhavati netarat.[47]

Both of the philosophies consider the Veda to be apauruṣeya, (impersonal) in the sense no person ever freely composed it.[48] There is also general agreement in the following matter among most of the followers of the different schools of Mīmāṁsā and Vedānta. "The entire Veda throws light only on what is not known through perception and inference. There is no need for scriptural quest in empirical matters".[49] "Scripture only directly informs about things unknowable otherwise, it neither produces anything new nor alters what is". "It does not have any authority to contradict knowledge from other sources; for instance, it cannot and does not state that 'fire is cold and wets things'." But its authority is inviolable in matters about which knowledge from other sources is impossible. As one means of knowledge (pramāṇa) cannot contradict another, even by a hundred examples scripture cannot and does not seek to disprove known facts.[50] Such is the clear and emphatic stand of Śaṅkarācārya in his own words. Rāmānujācārya concurs with this: "Perception apprehends things material; while scripture has as its object what is not determinable by perception etc. Thus there is no opposition between perception and scripture".[51] And, so does Madhvācārya: "Scripture ceases to be authoritative when it conflicts with experience".[52]

The implication of such a position should be laid bare: The Veda is, for example, neither *proved* if certain findings and theories of contemporary subatomic physics are shown to be in agreement with it, nor *disproved* if some developments and theories in contemporary molecular biology are shown to be not in agreement with it. Anything that could be *proved* or *disproved* by empirical experience, science or history, is not the purport, the core or essence, of the Veda. If something to be found in the Veda has so far been taken to be valid or true and if that is really and conclusively shown to be contradicted by empirical knowledge, it only proves that what was so far mistakenly taken as valid or true is not the purport of the Veda. If what has so far been taken to be the purport of the Veda is *demonstrated* to be valid and true by empirical knowledge, then also it cannot be the purport of the Veda, the function of which, if it were really the Veda as conceived by Mīmāṁsā-Vedānta, is to enlighten on matters beyond the ken of empirical knowledge. A redundant pramāṇa cannot be "the Veda". Meditation and contemplation on Vedic teaching can only remove any notion of its impossibility along with the notion of the possibility of its contradictory being true. The essence of the Veda has to be deliberated upon for years in a sustained way with faith by the pure mind of the one who has become an ethical being; then one may arrive at a certainty of its being truth, and, finally, one may 'realise' it. This is the classical stand.

IV

Attitudes to the Veda: Some Ancient Views

The disparagement of certain tendencies in the earlier portions of the Veda found in the later portions (viz., the Upaniṣads) is familiar to all who have read monographs on the latter or introductions to the translations of them.[53] It should also be remembered that they do also approvingly say that "this great unborn Self (eṣa mahān aja ātmā)—the Brāhmaṇas seek to know it by the study of the Veda".[54] It is not, however, widely known that there are a few passages in the saṁhitās like, for instance, the one which condemns mere hymn-reciters who wander about babbling as if covered in a mist.[55] Then in the sūkta praising the knowledge of the supreme Brahman, as Sāyaṇa explained, the mere reciters (pāṭhakas) who do not know the meaning of the Veda are condemned (nindyante).[56] The one who is ignorant of meaning even when seeing the Speech (of the Veda) does not see and even when hearing it does not hear, because he derives no advantage from that.[57] A mere reciter serves Speech bereft of flowers and fruits; he is like a dry log of wood which is fit only to be fuel. He can neither perform rituals, nor reach heaven. Dharma propounded in the earlier part of the Veda is the flower and Brahman-knowledge expounded in its later part is the fruit, which results in Brahman-realisation. For the mere reciter neither of these two is available. Also, a mere reciter has Speech which is unproductive, and is like one who possesses a fat barren cow which does not yield milk.[58] This is how that sūkta-composer, Yāska and Sāyaṇa thought about meaningless Vedapāṭha.

Pāraskara in his gṛhyasūtras informs that in his time those who planned to become priests just got the mantras by heart, while Ādityasena, a commentator on Laugākṣī gṛhya-sūtra mentions that many officiants at rituals knew only how to recite the mantras without knowing their meaning and that they even maintained it was useless to know it. Veṅkaṭa-Mādhava thought that even the authors of some kalpasūtras did not fully understand the mantras. Some smṛtis like Dakṣa, Auśanasa and Yājñavalkya had to exhort that one should not limit oneself to learn how to recite the Veda but also learn its meaning. All this means from very ancient times usually most learnt the Veda by rote without caring to know what it meant. Naturally, such reciters known as 'chāndasas' or śrotriyas were looked upon somewhat contemptuously, as is evident from literature. They were dubbed as "ignorant of the Veda" and as its "sellers".[59] For instance, the *Bhojacaritra* narrates that when some śrotriyas came to seek an audience with king Bhoja, himself a scholar-poet and a great patron of poetry, literature and scholarship, his chamberlains "laughing in fun at them" (kautukāt hasanto) went to the king and reported that "at the gate were standing chāndasas, enemies of poetry, with ugly discoloured teeth and their hands placed on their hips*".[60] This image of mere Vedapāṭhakas as lacking in commonsense, refinement, scholarship and proficiency in anything useful or productive, still by and large continues.

It is, therefore, not surprising that at a very early date the theory of the meaninglessness (ānarthakya) of the mantras, was formulated. As they are neither injunctions (vidhis), nor complementary to them, it was concluded, they were meaningless. They have only an elocutory value; just through utterance of them they become significant. A person named Kautsa advocated this view. Whether he is Kautsa Āṅgirasa,

* The *Sāhitya Darpaṇa* (I.2.) declares poetry superior to the Veda, for, its commentary explains, it is insipid, troublesome to learn and fit for aging intellects.

to whom an Ātharvaṇic prātiśākhya is attributed and the reputed teacher mentioned in the *Śatapatha* and some śrauta, dharma and gṛhya sūtras, or another person of that name, cannot be decided. If Āpadeva, a famous Mīmāṁsā writer, could hold the view that 'gods' have no existence apart from the mantras and that a 'god' is only a name inflected in the dative case in formulae (mantras) uttered while offering oblations,[61] an eminent ancient sage could have pronounced mantras to be senseless. The *Nirukta* and Mīmāṁsā[62] combated Kautsa's theory and upheld the meaningfulness (arthavattva) of mantras. Thus a process of mechanical ritualisation of the Veda was sought to be prevented by them.

What has been narrated happened in the dim past. Centuries later one Bhartṛmitra denied that the prescribed daily rituals as well as the prohibited acts have any good or bad results. Pārthasārathi Miśra has mentioned this.[63] It is possible that Kumārila had this teacher or such others in mind when he wrote that by his time Mīmāṁsā had almost become mechanical and materialistic (lokāyatīkṛtā) and that he was attempting to restore its original purity.

Tarka-Vyākaraṇa

I now come to 'Tarka-Vyākaraṇa'. Taking the first, early Nyāya maintained that the Veda is the work of reliable persons; while later Nyāya mentioned God as its author. The latter argued that the omniscient and compassionate creator of the world, who can be inferred, could not have left beings without teaching them the means of attaining the good. The teaching of this person, who is like a father of all, must have been preserved with great respect by the earliest beings. The Veda embodies that teaching. None else except an infinite omniscient being could have authored a work like the Veda as its contents are so unique, profound, all-embracing and consistent. The Veda, for Nyāya, is inerrant and free from contradictions. If it were not the authentic scripture it could have neither established the institution of four castes and four stages of life, nor would it have been acceptable to generations of good men from immemorial times till now. Reasoning cannot give the entire truth; it cannot establish what is 'good' or 'bad'. Any inference opposed to perception or the scripture is only an apparent inference. In the realm of dharma, Nyāya holds, reason is useful only in protecting the truth revealed by scripture from heresies, and has no positive role.[64]

The Vaiyākaraṇas claim that the purpose of grammar is (i) to protect (rakṣā) Vedic forms which must remain changeless; (ii) to provide appropriate words through conjecture (ūhā); (iii) to make available an easy method of grasping the language; and (iv) and to clear doubts.[65]

Sāṁkhya-Yoga

Now I come to 'Sāṁkhya-Yoga'. According to Kapila, the Veda is neither eternal, nor a product. No one could have produced it: for a person in bondage, lacking omniscience, could not have authored it, while a 'freed' person would not have a motive to do anything. The Veda itself says it is a product; so it cannot be eternal. The Veda came into existence spontaneously, like the grass and trees in a forest. Its validity is intrinsic and self-proved.[66] The *Sāṁkhyakārikā*, considered the oldest available work of this system, says for the complete eradication of suffering there is neither an empirical, nor an 'ānuśravika' means. 'Ānuśravika' is what is transmitted orally from person to person, generation to generation, continuously; and that is known through scripture, viz., the Veda. "Ānuśravika" means are defective, says the Kārikā, because (i) they are impure as in sacrifices, etc., they involve injury to beings, (ii) their effects (heavenly happiness, etc.), are impermanent, and (iii) they may create jealousy, etc., due to unevenness of their fruits. So, freedom from suffering, Sāṁkhya teaches, will be possible only through non-empirical and non-scriptural means.[67]

According to Yoga, God is the perfect person untouced by any defect whatsoever. Scriptures are the proof for this; and scriptures have their proof in the perfect quality of God's 'sattva' (principle of light and harmony). Both scriptures and perfection are present in God's sattva, and there is an eternal relation between the two. God having resolved to instruct all beings in right knowledge and dharma composed the scriptures, which are the expressions of God's perfect thought.[68]

Vaiśeṣika

I now come to the Vaiśeṣika. Sacred tradition, it says, is authoritative, because it is 'their teaching' (tadvacana). The authors' reliability guarantees its authority. The Veda is not eternal; it is the work of some persons or person. Nevertheless, it is authoritative, because it deals with dharma. Verbal testimony is not an independent means of knowledge, but really an inference from the reliability of its giver to the truth of what he says.[69]

Manusmṛti

No smṛti is closer to the Veda than that of Manu and no other is more acceptable than it to the zealous followers of the Veda, and no Hindu traditionalist of any school rated any other smṛti higher than it. The *Manusmṛti* has lavished the highest praise on the Veda, considering it to be the scripture *par excellence* and its authority and validity paramount. So, it is instructive to take note of what it has said on Vedic sacrifices and duties and what according to it is the highest act. In its second chapter occur these remarkable verses: "It is not good to have desire* (kāma); yet there is no desirelessness. But acceptance and study of the Veda as well as 'Vedic Karmayoga' is dependent on desire (or, arises from desire). The will is the root of desire, and sacrifices are generated by the will. All vows, religious observances, re-

* Another way to translate this is: It is not laudable to be desireful (desireful = in a state of having desires).

straints and dharmas are considered to be products of the will. In this world no action whatsoever of a desireless one is seen; whatsoever one does is the doing of desire. One who is *well-engaged* in actions goes to the immortal world, and, also, here he has all his desires fulfilled as willed by him".[70] To understand the implications of these and the nature of 'Vedic karmayoga' some verses in its last chapter have to be considered.

In its last chapter after saying all that has to be said on the rise of results of actions, the *Manusmṛti* continues as follows: "Now hear about the action which, for a brāhmin, produces the supreme good (naiḥśreyasa). Regular study of the Veda, askesis (tapas), knowledge, control of the senses, non-injury (ahiṁsā) and service of guru: this constellation is the highest in producing the supreme good. Now, here of all these auspicious actions, one is said to be the most productive of the supreme good for a human being. It is the knowledge of the self which is considered the best among them; it is the foremost of all knowledges (vidyās); and by that immortality is attained. Among these six actions Vedic action is to be cognised as action most conducive of good in life and after death. In the different components of 'Vedic karmayoga' all these are included one after another. Vedic action is twofold, involved (pravṛtta) and uninvolved (nivṛtta); from the former happiness and prosperity, and from the latter the supreme good are attained. Involved action is motivated by desire here and in the other world; while desireless action done with knowledge is taught to be uninvolved action. One who performs involved action becomes like gods, while one who performs uninvolved transcends the five elements (pañcabhūtas). Seeing the Self in all beings and all beings in the Self, thus seeing the Same (samam paśyan) the sacrificer of the self attains self-rule (svārājya). A superior brāhmin, even neglecting all the prescribed actions, ought to be diligently engaged in the knowledge of the self, tranquillity and regular study of the Veda".[71] In this smṛti-exposition may be found as good an exposition of the essence of Vedic religion as anywhere else, and the closeness of this 'Vedic karmayoga' to the karmayoga of the Bhagavadgītā. It succeeds in showing a way of understanding from a higher standpoint the apparent ritualistic religion of the earlier part of the Veda and relating it to the obvious spiritual teaching of the later part. This is what is important in this smṛti, and not its many verses about social organisation, the "do's" and "don'ts", the tabus, etc., which are irrelevant.

Mahābhārata

The *Mahābhārata* calls itself and a number of purāṇas like the *Brahmāṇda*, the *Skānda* and the *Śrīmadbhāgavata* also call it the fifth Veda. It is, indeed, an encyclopaedia of Hinduism. It says many things about the Veda at many places, often briefly. I am going to expound what is found in it at only three places.

The first is from the 'Pativratopākhyāna' (the Story of the Chaste Married Lady) in the Āraṇyakaparva: "It is very difficult to know the eternal dharma, which is established in truth. The elders laid it down that śruti is the authority for dharma. Dharma is subtle and appears in diverse ways. [It cannot be said that the actual nature of dharma becomes manifest just from a study of the Veda.] Although you are pure, a knower of dharma and engaged in study of the Veda, I think you do not know dharmas in their true nature". So admonishing, a chaste married lady advised a brāhmin to go to a righteous butcher to learn dharmas. In the teaching imparted by the butcher, the following appears to be a part of what is striking: "The essence of the Veda is truth, of truth sense-control (dama) and of the latter relinquishment (tyāga)" *. "Non-injury is the supreme dharma, and that is

* Elsewhere between dama & tyāga, tapas (askesis) is placed, and the final result of tyāga is said to be śama (tranquillity). ('Śukānupraśna', p. 2318).

established in truth. Having basis in truth, the inclinations of a good man proceed (or take from)". "The unsurpassed behaviour of the good has only three steps: do not harm, give and speak truth".

The second is from the 'Sanatsujātaparva' (the Teaching of Sanatsujāta) in the 'Udyogaparva': (1) A question was raised, "will one who has studied the three Vedas be defiled by the sins one has committed, because there are texts like 'one who is purified by the three Vedas becomes glorified in brahmaloka'?" The reply given was, "Neither singly nor together can the three Vadas save one from the sin of one's actions; I am not telling anything false. The Vedas cannot save a sinner or a deceitful one continuing to deceive. For the attainment of the Supreme Self the Veda has propounded tapas, sacrifice, etc., through which sin is destroyed and merit gained; then through the light of knowledge will come sākṣātkāra of the Supreme Self. Thus from knowledge only is the Self attained".[73] (2) There is no one who knows the Vedas; or there may be some rare one who knows their essence. He who knows only the Vedic sentences does not know what ought to be knowable through them. But he who firmly abides in truth knows what ought to be known through Vedic sentences.[74] (3) A question was asked, "who should be supposed to be a brāhmin, the one who knows the 5 Vedas, including itihāsas and purāṇas, or the one who knows 4 Vedas, 3, 2, 1 only, or not even 1? " The reply was: "As the One Veda was not known, many were made. In the essence of the One Veda of the nature of Truth rarely is someone found to be rooted. Without knowing at all the true nature of the Veda some suppose themselves to be great wise men. . . . The brāhmin who has read much is merely a well-read man; do not consider anyone who can just talk a lot a brāhmin. Only he who does not swerve from Truth is to be known as a brāhmin. Those who know the mantras but do not know what ought to be known from the Vedas, are not really knowers of them".[75]

The third is from the 'Kapilagosaṁvāda' in the Śāntiparva, which is actually a dialogue between Kapila and Syūmaraśmi. In order to know the truth, as the latter himself states, he submits for the former's consideration the thesis that the Vedic ideal is the married householder (gṛhastha) who (i) fulfils the duties pertaining to his caste and station in life, (ii) carries out the ritual and actions necessary for discharging the three debts which everyone owes*, and (iii) performs sacrifices**, the obligatory ones and also those which will take him to heaven; for (according to him) except through sacrifice heaven is impossible, and men, animals, plants, etc., all, desire heaven. Along with the sacrificed animals, etc., Syūmaraśmi continues, the sacrificer goes up to heaven. According to him, it is certain (i) that for the non-sacrificer there is neither this world nor the other, and (ii) that liberation is impossible without discharging the three debts. Only the gṛhastha, he thinks, does productive work (śrama), performs sacrifices and askesis and sustains the continuity of the human race as well as supports those who have become renunciants abandoning all productive work and rituals, because of their disbelief, foolishness, hopelessness, idleness or tiredness. Thus the position of the gṛhastha being the root of all dharma, how can it be true, Syūmaraśmi asks, that 'from the house liberation is impossible'? He further argues that according to śruti anything other than Vedic utterances cannot be śāstra. A man with family accomplishes something very difficult, for he is engaged in scriptural study, sacrifices, begetting and bringing up of children and cultivating straightforwardness (honesty, ārjava), while pursuing some occupation for the maintenance of himself and his family; and if, in spite of doing all this, he has not done all that ought to be done and, consequently, there is no liberation for him, Syūmaraśmi exclaims, then fie (dhik) upon such a doer,

---

* to gods, sages and manes.

** including those which may involve killing of animals.

what is done and such profitless labour ! He concludes: liberation or whatever is the ultimate good must be attainable by relying on Vedic utterances; not to admit this leads to nihilism (nāstikya) and violation of the Veda. Finally, he begs Kapila to comment on his thesis and enlighten him as to what really is welfare (nirāmaya) and eternity (ānantya). 'Nirṇaye kiṁ nirāmayam?" "Ānantyamicchāmi".[76]

Kapila, in response to the above, sets forth what he deems to be the correct Vedic position, which may be summarised as follows: The strivers (yatis) after the supreme state (parā gati) following the path of knowledge, sure in their mind, determined to relinquish and be liberated[77] and having relinquished, are freed from all desires, impurities, sin and grief, and devoted to Brahman, become It and are established in It.[78] There is no purpose in their becoming gṛhasthas.[79] While various rituals of the devout are several types of eternal worship,[80] the pure, steadfast and contented who have given up all action and have taken recourse to Brahman satisfy the gods by their knowledge of Brahman only. If one 'safeguards' one's hands and feet, speech, belly and sex organ*, one is a true brāhmin; if one has not done so, what can one do with askesis, sacrifice or oneself?[81] He, who with minimum necessary worldly possessions, lives in peace and contentment, knowing the nature of reality, and the causes and conditions of all that is happening and the destiny of beings, who is fearless of all and of whom all are fearless, and who has become the self of all beings, is a true brāhmin. Such a

* 'Safeguarding hands and feet' = not to play dice, not to take another's money, not to accept food of an inferior, and not to harm anyone in anger. 'Safeguarding speech' = not to abuse or curse anyone, not to lie, not to speak unnecessarily, not to spread rumours, to be devoted to truth and to be alert. 'Safeguarding belly' = neither to fast nor to eat too much, not to be greedy about food, and to eat only as much as is necessary to live. 'Safeguarding sex organ' = fidelity to one's own wife and to have intercourse even with her only during the days suitable for conception, and chastity.

person's conduct and behaviour is what truly reflects the Vedic norm; it is what interpenetrates all dharmas. Those who cannot conform to it consider actions conducive for treading the path of knowledge useless. As for other actions and rituals, *first,* it is difficult to understand their nature and procedure; *secondly,* even after understanding them it is very difficult to perform them; and, *lastly,* even after performing them one finds their fruits to be transient.[82] To the questions at the end of the last paragraph, Kapila's answers are: Whatever is performed according to śāstra results in welfare. Whoever follows the path of knowledge is purified, whoever goes astray from it is destroyed. Those who, not understanding śāstra and supported by argumentation and impelled by desire and aversion, become subject to egoism cannot achieve śāstraic knowledge, but cite śāstra to justify their position. They are, indeed, unbelievers in śāstra who 'rob the Veda';[83] they enter into darkness only. But the others who rightly understand śāstra see that involvement in the guṇas of prakṛti (basic stuff of the universe) results in being affected by aversion, desire, anger, falsehood and pride. So, strivers engaged in self-control, aiming at the supreme state, relinquish good and evil. 'Santyajeyuḥ śubhāśubhaṁ, parāṁ gatimabhīpsanto yatayaḥ saṁyame ratāḥ'.

Kapila continues and concludes thus: For all people the Vedas are the authority; they cannot and should not be violated. Both the Brahmans, i.e., Brahman in its verbal form and in its absolute nature (śabda- and para-brahman) are to be known; one who knows the former well would be able to know the latter. Actions done in the following manner indirectly lead to eternity. Those who perform sacrifices and other rituals without expecting anything, just because it is dharma to perform them, are freed from all passions, egoism and sins, obtain certain knowledge and hold fast to it, and work for the good of all beings. They are always content, happy, peaceful, sincere and honest, and conduct themselves according to the Vedas. There have been many like that, kṣatriyas, brāhmaṇas and others, who remained as gṛhasthas and never abandoned actions. They do attain everlastingness (ānantya), says the eternal śruti. Actions purify and knowledge liberates. The eternal dharma of the strivers which culminates in liberation may be practised independently by the renunciants, or conjointly with their duties by others in any station of life (as celibate-students, householders, or forest-dwellers).[84] Persons belonging to any caste or station in life can practise this safe and faultless dharma and attain eternity.[85] The one and same dharma is, indeed, fourfold (as the four āśramas), and everyone in any situation may follow it. Thus in the path of knowledge all āśramas are unified, and all castes are eligible for it. The paths to Brahman, the Supreme, are sincerity, patience, peace, non-injury, truth, straightforwardness, non-malice, non-arrogance, modesty, tolerance and tranquillity.[86] No human being is precluded from cultivating them. That which the happy and contented who possess these and have certain knowledge attain is the ultimate good, the supreme end. According to Kapila, while the Veda-knower is one who knows the Vedas and what is to be known through them, anyone else only emits 'gas'.[87] A Veda-knower knows everything, as everything is established in the Veda. Whatever is and is not has its basis in the Veda. What is known from and knowable in the Veda (Kapila finishes) is righteousness and truth, the Self of all, Brahman, which is the good established in total relinquishment (samastatyāga), tranquillity (śama) and contentment (santoṣa).[88]

The Kapila-Syūmaraśmi dialogue has been given considerable space because through Kapila the author-editor of the *Mahābhārata,* as we have it now, seems to express his view on the Vedic teaching. It tallies with the contents of many other dialogues in this great epic (e.g., of Nārada-Gālava, Parāśara-Janaka, Haṁsa-Sādhyas, Yājñavalkya-Viśvāvasu, and even of Śukānupraśna, Manubṛhaspati,[89] etc.) and it does not differ much from what the *Bhagavadgītā* says.

Taking into account the reputation of the *Mahābhārata* as the 'fifth Veda' as well as its comprehensiveness and profundity, its attitude to the Vedas and its account of their contents have to be taken as seriously as those of, *e.g.*, Mīmāṁsā, and have to be given much more weight than modern Western and Indian works on Vedic philosophy, religion, or spirituality/mysticism, and perhaps, than even the Veda bhāṣyas now available. According to one of the greatest Vedāntic teachers, Madhvācārya, God descended into the world as Vyāsa and composed the *Mahābhārata* which elaborates the entire meaning of the Veda as well as that which though not contained in the Veda is the object of the absolute knowledge of God. On the basis of Purāṇic statements Madhva asserted that the *Mahābhārata* is not only the fifth Veda, but is also superior to the other four Vedas. (Madhva's introductory bhāṣya on the Gītā) Those who accept the authority of itihāsa-purāṇas cannot brush off what a number of them said about the Veda and about themselves. It may be remembered that Śaṅkarācārya and others quoted purāṇic and Gītā passages and stated them to be from smṛtis. So, they were, accorded smṛti status by the great Vedāntic ācāryas too.

Rāmāyaṇa

The second great Indian epic, Vālmīki's *Rāmāyaṇa*, is considered to contain the essence of Vedānta. Vaiṣṇavas of the school of Rāmānujācārya believe it to be (i) an interpretation of the dvaya-mantra[90] (twofold mantra) which teaches about both what is to be attained and what leads one to it, the means and the end, the choosing of the means and self-dedication to the Divine;[91] and (ii) an explanation of the Gāyatrī-mantra, which is believed to be the essence of the Veda. Ācāryas of that school as well as a commentator of the *Rāmāyaṇa*, Govindarāja, have endeavoured to show this in their writings. For the Vaiṣṇavas it is a long scripture on the doctrine and practice of surrender to the Supreme Person (dīrghaśaraṇāgati-grantha). Without going into all that, I will refer only to what this epic says about the Veda in two places.

(1) In the 'Ayodhyākāṇḍa', in the course of rebutting a materialistic position which also denied scriptural authority, Rāma is described as having said the following: "The universe is established in Truth. The highest dharma is Truth. Truth is the lord of the Universe.* All have their roots in Truth. There is no position or abode higher than Truth. The Vedas have their foundation in Truth (or, they have their glory due to it). 'Vedāḥ satyapratiṣṭhānāḥ'. Therefore, one should be devoted to Truth."[92]** This implies the Veda teaches truth and hence its authority. (2) In the 'Yuddhakāṇḍa' occurs (four-faced) Brahmā's laudation of Rāma in the course of which we find, among others, these utterances: "You are Nārāyaṇa, the immutable Brahman, the eternal Truth, the ultimate Dharma, the Supreme Person, the Creator. You are of the nature of (or the very self of) the thousand-branched [Sāma] Veda, the teacher in various ways of the dharma of diverse types and the best among the best. 'Sahasraśṛṅgo Vedātmā śatajihvo maharṣabhaḥ.' The Vedas are your breath. There is nothing that can be without you. 'Saṁskārāste' bhavanvedā na tadasti tvayā vinā'.[93] It may be concluded that, according to the *Rāmāyaṇa*, the source of the Veda is the immortal divine Person and it teaches the saving truth.

Bhāgavata

Among the purāṇas, one of the most, if not *the* most, profound and spiritual is the *Śrīmad Bhāgavata*. What it says about the Veda is most interesting. In the chapters of its middle skandha dealing with the Ajāmila story, this purāṇa contrasts the dharma of the three Vedas dependent on the guṇas*** with the pure "Bhāgavata dharma" (dharma of

* The passage could justifiably be also translated as "God is Truth".

** From this can be seen the antiquity of the idea of the identification of Truth-Supreme Reality-God, often expressed by Mahatma Gandhi.

*** fundamental qualities/constitutive elements of all things, sattva, rajas and tamas.

loving devotion to God, or bhakti-yoga);[94] and comments thus: "Alas, most of these great men, deluded by divine māyā, do not know that bhakti-yoga consisting of utterance of divine names, etc., is the highest dharma; and that the glorification through recitation of God's qualities, actions and names, is entirely sufficient for the removal of sin. So, with their intellect dulled by the flowery honeyed language of the three Vedas they get involved in huge empty rituals."[95] This is a disvaluation of Vedic ritualism.

A chapter in the tenth skandha of the *Bhāgavata* is concerned with the problem, how can the śrutis conditioned by guṇas (guṇa-vṛttayaḥ) deal with Brahman, indescribable and without guṇas, which is beyond existence and non-existence? The problem is sought to be resolved by narrating a gāthā (legend) of personified Vedas lauding God to wake him up at the end of the dissolution of the world (pralaya)! Known as "Vedastuti"(Vedic Laud), it consists of 28 ślokas expounding a number of mostly Upaniṣadic sentences in a quite original way. They are supposed to show how the śrutis deal with Brahman. But here, to illustrate the attitude of this purāṇa to the Veda, I would only provide the translation of an introductory verse before the beginning of the gāthā and of the very last verse of this chapter, which comes after the gāthā is finished and extolled. *First,* the former: (1) "This Upaniṣad related to Brahman was borne (dhṛtā) in mind by the primordial ancestors; whoever bears it likewise with faith reaches 'kṣema' (lit. security, felicity; i.e., highest state), having nothing (i.e., freed from conditions, upādhis)".[96] Here we find the real śrutis are impliedly taken to be the Upaniṣads only and it is attempted to show how they are able to talk about the Absolute. In another śloka the portion of the Veda which praises rituals, though accepted as God's word, is dismissed as confusing the obtuse.[97] *Now the last śloka:* "One should constantly meditate on Hari, the absolutely free and fearless, devoid of māyā (the world-cause). The origination, sustenance and dissolution of this universe are His projective imaginative willing. He is the lord of the unmanifest (avyakta, prakṛti) and souls (jīvas). Having projected all this, He entered into it along with the Jīva as its self and made different kinds of bodies and governs them. Just as one in deep sleep does not attend to one's body, a jīva who attains Him becomes free from māyā."[98] Here the ultimate goal is propounded as the Free and the Fearless* conceived as the Supreme Person, the creator and lord through His illusory power which is the material cause of the universe, by meditating on whom one attains Him and transcends the effect of His illusory power. This is presented as the essence of "Vedastuti".

Finally, in its last but one skandha, in a chapter dealing with forest-dwellers and renunciants, the *Bhāgavata* lays down that "one should neither be an addict to 'Vedavāda' (Vedic disputation or discussion), a heretic, or a mere logician, nor adopt any position in 'dry' controversies and argumentations".[99] It is surprising 'Vedavāda' is put on a par with heresy, sophistry and fruitless argumentation, although in the context of prohibitions for those in the last two stages of life. Apparently, this prohibited 'Vedavāda' is not discussion and meditation on the meaning of Upaniṣadic sentences, but is about the contents of the portion of the Veda dealing with 'vaitānika mahat karma (huge empty ritual), which dulls and confuses (jaḍīkaroti) one's intellect. 'Vedavāda' like 'Brahmavāda' cannot be at all taken as pejorative when it is not endless argumentation about how different rituals are to be performed and what the specific 'intention' (abhiprāya, saṁkalpa) of each is. In such cases it is legitimate reasoning with a view to ascertain truth and assimilate it.

The Gītā

I have reserved to the last consideration of the attitude of

---

* cp. What Yājñavalkya made known to Janaka was the Fearless. After receiving the upadeśa (teaching) the king told the sage, "You have made the Fearless known to us. Salutations to you". "Yo no bhagavannabhayaṁ vedayase; namaste'stu". *Bṛhadāraṇyaka Upaniṣad*, IV.2.4.

the *Bhagavadgītā* to the Veda, as it may be taken to be the conclusive Hindu position, because although the Gītā forms part of the *Mahābhārata* it has been more or less treated as an independent śāstra, and its authority is held to be next only to the śruti and superior to all other works by almost all the ācāryas. In the introductory portion of his commentary to it Śaṅkarācārya has declared that the Gitāśāstra being the summary of the substance of the meaning of the entire Veda is difficult to be comprehended'.[100] In his *Brahmasūtrabhāṣya* he quoted the *Gītā* 42 times, and Rāmanujācārya in his quotes it 104 times.

In 6 of its 18 chapters something or other is said about the Veda. In the II chapter 8 ślokas are devoted to it; in XI and XV in each 3; in VIII, IX and XIII in each 2; and only 1 in XVII. The two last ślokas in XVI virtually refer to it. All these will be considered now.

The Veda is brought into the discourse for the first time in the following manner. In a certain context the *Gītā* starts by asserting that purposeful and decisive thinking is one-pointed, while purposeless and indecisive thinking is many-branched and endless. Then it goes on thus (freely translated): Addicted to Vedic disputation (Vedavāda), the unwise utter flowery language arguing that there is nothing more. Covetous, intent on heaven, involved in seeking pleasures and power, they are robbed of their intelligence by the flowery language which yields only rebirth and the fruit of actions and is full of various rituals aiming at pleasures and power. For such people establishment of one-pointed thinking in enstasis (samādhi) is impossible. It continues: The sphere of the Vedas is that of the three guṇas;* become free from the

* "Traiguṇyaviṣayā Vedāḥ" is explained by Śaṅkara as "traiguṇyaṁ saṁsāro viṣayaḥ prakāśayitavyo yeṣām te vedāḥ traiguṇyaviṣayāḥ". It means: the subject-matter of the Vedas is what is constituted by the three guṇas, the phenomenal world, on which they shed light. To be free from guṇas, he wrote, is to be free from desire (niṣkāma).

latter, as well as from the pairs of opposites and from acquisition and possession, and, always abiding in purity, be self-possessed. All the Vedas, the passage concludes, are of as much use to an enlightened brāhmin as a tank is to anyone in a place flooded with water on all sides.[101]

The last sentence is explained by Śaṅkarācārya thus: Vedic works have endless fruits. Whatever profit is in them is included in the profit which a renunciant knower of the absolute reality gains through his knowledge. Śaṅkara takes the metaphor in the verse to mean: small containers of water like wells, tanks, etc., have only limited uses (bathing, drinking, etc.), but a huge full reservoir of water is of unlimited use. For example, it can in addition to catering to the needs of bathing, drinking, etc., provide for the irrigation of huge tracts of land. The bliss of Brahma-jñāna (Brahman-knowledge) includes the fuits of all possible good actions/rituals. In support of this interpretation Śaṅkara quotes a śruti text, "Whoever knows That obtains the fruits of all the good works that people may perform", and a *Gītā* text, "All action without remainder culminates in knowledge".[102] The latter text significantly follows these statements: (i) knowing that all kinds of sacrifices spring from action, one becomes free, and (ii) the sacrifice of knowledge (jñāna-yajña) is superior to that of things (dravya-yajña).

Different but no less enlightening is Rāmānujācārya's explanation of the same sentence: "A thirsty man should drink from a tank only as much water as he needs and not all that is in it. Like that, to a follower of the Vedas who seeks liberation, in all the Vedas only that which is the means to liberation must be acceptable, not anything else in them."[103] This implies that although all the Vedas contain besides the means to liberation what is not so, a believer in Vedic authority desiring liberation should accept only what is conducive to it.

Chapter II of the Gītā contains two more important verses on scriptural authority: "(i) When your thinking becomes free from the pollution of delusion (indiscrimination),* then you will become indifferent** to "What is to be heard and what has been heard in the Veda (śrotavyasya śrutasya ca). (2) When your thinking distracted by the śruti becomes immovable and steadfast in enstasis, then you will attain yoga (discriminative insight)***."[104] For one free from 'pollution' mentioned in the former verse, Śaṅkara explains, the yet to be heard and the already heard from the Veda become infructuous. "Tadā śrotavyaṁ śrutaṁ ca niṣphalaṁ pratipadyate iti abhiprāyaḥ." He further adds: The śrutis throw light on the relations between many ends and means. By hearing them thinking becomes distracted; but the wavering of the mind due to this must be stopped in order to steady it. "Anekasādhya-sādhanasaṁbandhaprakāśana-śrutibhiḥ śravaṇaiḥ vipratipannā nānāpratipannā vikṣiptā satī. . . ."[105]

All this does not mean that the *Gītā* does not accept the authority and validity of the Veda. It does so very much. In chapter XVI after distinguishing between the divine and demonic types among men, in the last two verses of it, according to Śaṅkarācārya, the *Gītā* teaches that 'only by relying on the authority of śāstra it is possible to abandon the demonic lot and adopt good conduct (śreyācaraṇa); so for both śāstra is the cause'. These two verses are: "(1) whoever throws away the injunctions of śāstras and lives wantonly, will not attain perfection, happiness or the ultimate goal. (2) Therefore, let śāstras be your authority in determining what is duty and what is not. It is appropriate for you to act with a knowledge of the dictates of śāstras".[106]

As śāstras can be only those which are the sources of the

---

* 'mohakalilaṁ mohātmakam avivekarūpaṁ kāluṣyaṁ', Śaṅkara. Indiscrimination is of the self from the not-self.

** nirvedaṁ vairāgyaṁ (unattachment), Śaṅkara.

*** yogaṁ vivekaprajñāṁ, Śaṅkara.

knowledge of what is duty and what is not,* and as only they can properly prescribe or prohibit any actions, obviously the Vedas are śāstras *par excellence*. They certainly are meant in the two verses. To the extent the smṛtis and itihāsa-purāṇas supplement and amplify what is in the Vedas, the former too are śāstras. The *Gītā* claims its own teaching to be śāstra;[107] as already said, Śaṅkara refers to the *Gītā* as a śāstra. The *Brahma-sūtra* refers to it as a smṛti;[108] in his sūtra-bhāṣya Śaṅkara quotes from the *Kūrma-purāṇa* stating the citation is from a smṛti.[109] I do not propose to discuss here the problem of "śruti-dvaidha" (conflict of Vedic precepts), apparent or actual, and contradictions (seeming or otherwise) between śrutis and other śāstras or among the latter. But the *Gītā* has itself provided a solution for that: "One ought to take refuge in one's own reason".[110] After completing his teaching, the divine teacher of the *Gītā* advised: "Reflecting** on this fully, do as you wish to do."[111] These principles as well as what the *Gītā* has said about the Veda in its several chapters, provide a useful guide to determine which is a śāstra and which is not and to what extent a śāstra is to be followed. Detailed discussions of this occur in the *Mahābhārata* and other works.

The justification for the critique of the Veda in chapter II of the *Gītā* has been given there itself, as already explained. In two verses of chapter IX some of this is reiterated more clearly. The first verse affirms that the performers of Vedic 'soma' sacrifices worship the One God through them, and purified from sin do go to heaven and enjoy celestial delights. *But,* the next verse after pointing out that through such enjoyment when their merit is exhausted, they come back to the mortal world, concludes that devotees of the

---

* kartavyākartavya, what ought to be done and what ought not to be, Śaṅkara.

** 'Vimṛśya', the text reads. Śaṅkara explains: 'Vimarśanaṁ ālocanaṁ kṛtvā'. Vimarśa = examination; consideration; reflection, discussion. (Macdonell's Dictionary)

dharma of the three Vedas who crave for the objects of desires and practise it manage only going up to heaven and coming down to earth, but do not obtain any kind of freedom.[112] Here and at other places too the *Gītā* admits that like charity and askesis, sacrifices do purify, but its considered and definite opinion is that they ought to be performed without attachment and abandoning fruits.[113] It also broadens the concept of sacrifice (yajña) and teaches that the best sacrifice is that of knowledge, because as already referred to, all other sacrifices spring from action and cannot lead to freedom.[114] Real sacrificial action is well-performed action without attachment, and that liberates*;[115] all other action binds. So, in the *Gītā* whenever the śruti, Vedas or the dharma of the three Vedas, appears to be disvalued or disparaged, the reference is only to Vedic ritualism performed in a mechanical way solely for fulfilling desires here or in heaven. The teaching in the portions of the Veda other than those which deal with this is not different from that of the *Gītā*. This becomes clear from the following citations:

> The supreme Imperishable (akṣara, Brahman) which the Veda-knowers proclaim, which the men of self-control freed from passion attain, desiring which brahmacarya (life of chastity, truth and study) is practised—that is what Bhagavān Kṛṣṇa** briefly declared to Arjuna. The yogi who knows well Brahman, the individual soul, etc., transcending the fruits of the merit mentioned in the Vedas, sacrifices, askesis and charity, goes to the highest state.[116]
>
> The highest form of God, described in chapter XI, was shown to Arjuna by God being pleased (prasannena), but no one else in the mortal world can behold it by the Vedas, sacrifices, study, charity, rituals or intense askesis. Only by exclusive devotion (bhaktyā

* 'Yajñārtha karma' is 'karma' of 'muktasaṅga', which must be 'samācarita'.
** Hereafter I use the term 'God' for Him.

ananyayā) God in that form can be known and seen in truth, and entered into.[117]

The true nature of the body and self has been chanted by the ṛṣis in various ways; in several ṛk and other Vedic metres in a discriminative way; and in the reasoned decisive sentences indicating Brahman found in the Upaniṣads.[118]

The peepul tree (the transmigratory world, 'saṁsāra') has an upward root* (Brahman) and downward branches (cosmic intellect, egoism, subtle elements, etc.) It is called imperishable (because though it** is undergoing destruction every moment, it has been in existence from beginningless time and sustains the beginningless and endless series of bodies, etc.). The Vedas are its leaves (for, like leaves which protect a tree, they protect the world by revealing dharma and not-dharma, as well as their causes and results). He who knows this tree (of saṁsāra along with its root, Brahman) is a knower of the Veda (he knows the meaning of the Veda).[119]

Only God is to be known through all Vedas; He is the maker of the Upaniṣads and the knower of the Veda.[120] Since He transcends the changing and is superior to the changeless, He is well-known in the world and the Veda as the Supreme Person.[121]

Oṁ Tat Sat is the threefold designation of Brahman.*** With it of old brāhmins, Vedas and sacrifices

---

* Its root (Brahman) is called 'upward' (ūrdhvaṁ) because of its causality, eternity and greatness. (Śaṅkara).

** Its name in Sanskrit 'asvattha' actually means what will not last even till tomorrow (na śvaḥ api sthātā). (Śaṅkara)

*** According to Rāmānuja Brahman here means the Veda. The Veda is śabda-brahman, the Absolute in verbal form. But Upaniṣadic sentences like "Oṁ iti brahma (Oṁ is Brahman), Tattvamasi (That Thou art) and Sadeva..idamagra āsīt (*Sat* alone was this in the beginning)", show these words are designations of Brahman. (*Tai.* 1.8.1. Cha .6.8.7; 6.2.1).

were ordained. The Brahman-discussants* after pronouncing *Oṁ* undertake, as prescribed, acts of sacrifice, charity and askesis. The seekers of liberation pronounce *Tat* (That) and then undertake the same acts without coveting their fruits. *Sat* means the real, the good as well as any praiseworthy action. Action meant for, as well as steadfastness in, sacrifice, askesis and charity is also called *Sat*; but if these are without faith they are *Asat* (not-*sat*).[122]

These citations and the preceding discussion of the critique of the Vedas, śruti and trayīdharma found in the *Gītā* show its assessment of the Veda, which may be taken to represent the most authoritative traditional Hindu attitude to the latter. Considering that not only the Vedāntic ācāryas, but also great Māheśvaras like Abhinava Gupta, Yogis like Jñāneśvara and others from Kashmir to Dakṣiṇāpatha, and from the followers of Rāmānanda in the middle of India to those of Caitanya in the east of India, have venerated and expounded the *Gītā*, it is justified to hold this opinion.

V
Epitome

The previous section has provided a diversity of views regarding the Veda. Starting with what later parts of the Veda have said about its earlier parts and mere recitation of it, and after referring to the views of some sūtras, smṛtis and literary works, as well as of Kautsa and Bhartṛmitra, it has briefly outlined the views of four darśanas (philosophical systems) and Vyākaraṇa. The positions of the two Mīmāṁsās (pūrva, prior, and uttara, later) are *passim* in the first chapter and earlier sections of this chapter. These are followed by presenting the perspectives offered by the *Manusmṛti*, the *Mahābhārata*, the *Rāmāyaṇa*, *Śrīmadbhāgavata* and the *Bhagavadgītā*.

* Brahmavādinaḥ = those who study and expound the Veda, Śaṅkara.

The various views may be classified as follows. There were (i) those who thought the Veda contained only gibberish, but potent when uttered, a ridiculous theory; (ii) those who held that its injunctions and prohibitions have no moral effects, a theory which would be correct only if all action has no moral effect; (iii) those who rejected its authority on the ground that only sense perception and inference can be the sources of truth; and (iv) those who would admit the teachings of the omniscient too to be sources of valid knowledge, but deny omniscient authorship to the Veda. Of these, (i) would make the Veda a collection of incantations and (ii) would make morality meaningless. (iii) would be the position of the Lokāyatas or Cārvākas and (iv) that of the Jainas and Buddhists; (iii) is an intelligible viable position if transcendence (the trans-empirical, paraṁ) is denied; for the irreligious and the atheistic can be congruent (of course, not necessarily) with the moral, while the religious and the theistic are also not necessarily so*. But, *pace* Gauḍapāda and Udayana or Jābāli and Cārvī**, on logical or scientific grounds transcendence can be neither proved nor disproved; while its denial can be demolished, and argumentative affirmation of it can be destroyed. Curiously, all the adhārmic (non-moral) men indulging in evil actions (duṣkṛta) whom Rāma and Kṛṣṇa fought and destroyed were neither atheistic, nor avaidic. They were worshippers of (four-faced) Brahmā or Śiva, performers of Vedic rites and askesis. Hanūmān found fire-sacrifices and Vedic chanting in the houses of all the demons (rākṣasas) in Laṅkā. Moreover, the atheistic need not be necessarily irreligious (e.g., some Mīmāṁsakas, Jainas, etc.). Regarding (iv) it has been ably argued (but not demonstrated) that there cannot be an omniscient being and as such the teachings of 'tīrthaṅkaras' and

---

* What is spoken of here is logical necessity.

** Jābāli was one of the 'best brāhmaṇas' who denied transcendence: "Sa nāsti paramityeva kuru buddhiṁ", he taught. (*Rāmāyaṇa*, II.108.17) Cārvī was a teacher of Lokāyata (*Kāśikā Vṛtti*, I.3.36)

'tathāgatas' have no validity; while, *per contra*, it has been ably argued (but not demonstrated) that an eternal impersonal collection of sentences (as the Veda is claimed to be by some) is an impossibility and, on the other hand, that God being a myth there can be no scripture with divine authorship. Both these positions have been logically assaulted in forcible ways, but not knocked to pieces; they both thrive!

Of the four philosophical systems considered in this chapter, the Nyāya is the one which sought to defend logically Vedic authority and knowledge. Warding off possible criticism that the Veda suffers from the defects of falsity, contradiction and repetition,[123] it developed ingenious apologetic argumentation to refute it. Knowledge of truth, generated by enstasis (samādhi) preceded by ethico-psychological discipline,[124] has to be fully developed through apprehension, constant study and meditation of it and through dialogues with the adepts in it,[125] and this steady development and application of knowledge of truth has to be protected against the arguments of opponents not only by reasoning (tarka) such as *reductio ad absurdum* and disucssion (vāda) using syllogisms, but, if necessary, even by wrangling (jalpa) and cavilling (vitaṇḍā). The process of constant study, meditation and dialogues, Nyāya explains, is for removing doubts, and the use of argumentation, including extreme types of it, is for protecting the growing knowledge which has to attain unshakeable assured certainty. The use of jalpa and vitaṇḍā is like putting a fence of thorny branches around seedlings, says Gotama.[126]

Tattvajñāna (knowledge of truth) has to be fostered, Nyāya contends, by sustained thinking and logic. The place of tarka in understanding Vedic truth according to Nirukta and both the Mīmāṃsās has been elucidated in earlier sections of this chapter. Vācaspati's dictum Vedānta Mīmāṁsā is verily tarka has also been quoted there. Vyākaraṇa, which claims to have protection of the Veda as its aim, gives an important role to conjecture and analysis of sentences for understanding them and removing doubts. Sāṁkhya grants the Veda validity, but restricts its authority by asserting it to be a source of knowledge of defective means which give us temporary relief from suffering. For Vaiśeṣika all verbal knowledge being virtually inferential knowledge, the Veda is not really an independent source of knowledge. Pūrva Mīmāṁsā, Sāṁkhya and Vaiśeṣika systems do not seem to have given a place for God during much of their histories; while Nyāya asserted that God's existence may be logically proved. Even for tattvajñāna necessary for liberation, according to Śāṁkhya, Yoga, Nyāya and Vaiśeṣika systems, it is viveka (discrimination), samādhi (enstasis), or niṣkāma karma (desireless action) respectively which are necessary, not the Veda. But *all* these accepted the Veda as the source of dharma. Consequently, as an impure mind is unfit for discrimination, etc., and as for purifying it dharmic life has to be led, the importance of the Veda for the followers of all these systems is obvious. According to Mīmāṁsā, due performance of all daily and occasional duties prescribed by the Veda for their own sake, without any desire, leads one to liberation. So arises its total reliance on the Veda. Depending upon different schools of Vedānta, either pure knowledge of the Supreme Self, or knowledge of it which has assumed the form of loving devotion of Him (bhaktirūpāpannaṁ jñānaṁ), is the cause of liberation. As such knowledge arises either directly from the sentences of the last part of the Veda, or from sentences such as those of the smṛti-purāṇa-itihāsas dependent upon them, the Veda is for the Vedāntic systems the ultimate source of saving knowledge. That knowledge again is the fruit of a good life and pure mind; and only from the Veda can be learnt how to lead a good life. Thus the classical Vedāntic schools totally relied on śruti. So, as far as the classical philosophical systems are concerned, it is not correct to think, as Renou, did, that only external homage or substanceless adoration to the Veda became more usual in due course.[127]

It is not so much the darśanas, but the smṛti-itihāsa-purāṇas which influenced the life and thought of the people; and as the Vedāntic systems accepted the authority of the latter they were able to acquire gradually more power to affect people than the other systems. But, as already made clear in this section and what preceded it, none of these philosophical systems or Nirukta underrate reason, logic and argument. In this they follow the Veda itself. The *Ṛgveda* itself enjoined that "one should conform to one's own wisdom and attain with one's own mind even more excellent capacity." Uta svena kratunā saṁvadeta śreyāṁsaṁ dakṣaṁ manasā jagrubhyāt. (*Ṛgveda*, X. 20). There are a number of Upaniṣadic texts which emphasise that the Supreme has to be after all apprehended/known by reason/mind, purified by leading an ethical life and made sharp and fit by deep thinking, argument, discussion, dialogue and debate, with the motive of ascertaining truth. Cintana (reflection) on the meaning of Upaniṣadic sentences ought to be a life-long activity for any Brahman-seeker, according to Vedānta. Naturally, the great classical Vedāntic systems, which rely on the Upaniṣads, are rational systems, in the sense they cannot and do not accept as truth anything that contradicts empirical experience, science and history. Such is the case with Mīmāṁsā and Nyāya also; Sāṁkhya and Vaiśeṣika give even more scope to reason and Yoga to individual inner experience. The absurd cannot be true according to any classical Indian Philosophy.*

If we take a look at the *Manusmṛti*, the *bete noir* for some Hindu social reformers and revolutionaries, which in its present form does contain much that outrages civilised modern sensitive persons (some of which appears to have

* Whatever is said in this paragraph about Vedānta, Yoga, etc., is only about those darśanas as presented in the sūtras, bhāṣyas, and writings of thinkers like Kumārila and Vācaspati, and not about what is expounded as vedānta or yoga in later medieval or modern works.

been incorporated in it by the unscrupulous later at different periods), its emphasis on good sense and logic is clear; and in the light of that, the principles it itself sets forth and the universal values it upholds, all that is revolting in it can and should be discarded. This has to be done even in the case of bloody sacrifices* and such other things which are to be found in the Veda itself, which have been condemned outright in many contexts in the *Mahābhārata, Śrīmadbhāgavata***, etc. As said in the first chapter, scriptures of all religions and great classics of other cultures also contain obsolete, reprehensible and revolting material***, but the pure gold in them has to be separated from the dross with which it is mixed.

The enlightened portion of the *Manusmṛti*, which I like to take as authentic and original and the only one of relevance at present, does not advocate Vedic fundamentalism, but declares: "One who wishes *purification of dharma* (dharmaśuddhi) must very well know perception, inference and many branches of knowledge. Only he who is able to apply reasoning (tarka) not opposed to the Veda-śāstra to the Veda as well as to the teaching of dharma by the ṛṣis, will be able to know dharma, not anyone else".[128] It also contains this principle: "Any (so-called) dharma which will not later

---

* Traditional authorities assert that the Veda does not countenance human sacrifice at all. 'Puruṣamedha' and 'Sarvamedha', according to them, do not at all involve any injury to human beings. (Mm. Chinnaswami Sastri, *Yajñatattvaprakāśa*, reprinted in his *Janmaśatābdasmārakagrantha*, ed. Mandana Mishra and others, Varanasi, 1990, pp. 105-06). But some modern scholars think those are human sacrifices.

** What has been just said about the *Manusmṛti* is applicable to all smṛti-itihāsa-purāṇas.

*** e.g., Ideas like all non-Greeks are barbarians and slavery is justifiable in some Greek classics; thinking of African blacks as subhuman beings by Hume, Kant and others; glorification of the West and denigration of the East by many European thinkers, of the Prussian military State as the ideal by Hegel, of the superman by Nietzsche; and anti-Jewish tendencies in some communist works.

result in happiness and which is (generally) condemned in the world (lokavikruṣṭa) must be abandoned".[129] Another great smṛti, that of Yājñavalkya, confirms this, "A (so-called) dharma hated by the world (lokavidviṣṭa) must not be practised".[130] According to the *Mahābhārata*, actions opposed by the people (lokaviruddha) are as sinful as those condemned by the Veda (Vedaviruddha).[131]

It is significant that in reply to the question, how should one behave when the world is in total dhārmic confusion and ethical pollution?[132] The *Mahābhārata* advises: A wise man with controlled mind should rely on reason to decide what is dharma and what is not.[133] The *Bhagavadgītā* expressly enjoins: "Take refuge in reason".[134]

The *Manusmṛti* does not also promote Vedic exclusiveness. Even the entire Veda is not the sole source of dharma, it says, but a source along with (a) the smṛtis and (b) conduct of its knowers, as well as (c) the conduct of the good and (d) the glad satisfaction of oneself (ātmanastuṣṭi).[135] It is important to note that in addition to the first two, it mentions two more factors, implying that the good may not be the Veda-knowers only and that what is taken to be Vedic teaching must also appeal to and satisfy an individual. The good in the world or a country constitute a much larger number than that of the Veda-knowers; the first includes the second. This smṛti goes on to say that the character of dharma is fourfold: the Veda, smṛti, the conduct of the good and what is pleasing to oneself (priyamātmanaḥ).[136] It goes without saying that 'the glad satisfaction of oneself' or 'what is pleasing to oneself' cannot be also the exclusive source or character of dharma. Of course, for those inquiring into dharma, it ordains, the ultimate authority is śruti.[137] But, another significant thing in this connection is the chapter in which these verses occur begins with a definition of dharma which does not refer to the Veda! "Dharma is that which the wise and the good, without attachment and aversion, always practised, and which they acknowledged heartily (hṛdayenābhayanujñāta) as dharma".[138] It is difficult to think of a more enlightening and progessive definition of dharma. As this is followed by the other verses already cited, one may venture to conclude that what is cumulatively defined by all these verses put together is the Vaidika dharma.

I will now refer to a problematic issue which the *Mahābhārata* raises in connection with Vedic authority, and solves it. The issue is posed as follows: The knowers of śāstras have determined the Veda as the pramāṇa (the right means of knowledge) of dharma. But there is a decrease (hrāsa) of Vedic utterances from aeon to aeon*. Dharmas differ from aeon to aeon**. The system of dharmas in each aeon seems to depend on the capacities of human beings, which change from aeon to aeon. "What āmnāyas (traditions/sacred texts) say is true", seems to be a platitude for the propitiation of mankind. The Vedas are superior to āmnāyas and are projected universally. If all of them are pramāṇa, then there is no pramāṇa. If pramāṇa and apramāṇa are mutually contradictory, then from where is the śāstraness of which?[139] Such is the problematic put forward, which expressed in a simpler form would be: If dharmas are not the same from age to age and the pramāṇa for all of them, the one Veda, is also changing, can it still be the source of eternal truth? How can mutually-contradictory traditions, some of which also contain what is opposed to the Veda, together with the Veda, or each of them be pramāṇa? The *Mahābhārata* answers this through a declaration of the principal character of a story it narrates: "I know the dharma

---

* This may mean one of these: (i) The decisions of the Veda regarding dharma change from aeon to aeon. Or (ii) the corpus of the Veda is infinite, but from aeon to aeon starting after the Kṛta what is available of it to mortals becomes more and more limited, thus resulting in a virtual shrinking of it.

** The *Manusmṛti* says exactly the same: The first three pādas of its I. 85., and the first three of the *Mahābhārata*, XII. 252. 8., are identical except for one word. In the smṛti the last word in the third pāda is "nṛṇāṁ", but in the other it is "dharmā".

eternal with its secret, ancient, good and friendly for all beings. To live without malice, or at least with minimum malice, towards beings is the supreme dharma".[140] Thus the fifth Veda in one sentence enunciates an admirable principle by conforming to which dhārmic life would be possible. It can and should be followed in all ages and situations, and is thus an eternal law. It is as ridiculous to consider patterns of social order and mores like varṇāśrama (caste and station in life), and untouchability as eternal dharma as it is to consider slavery, apartheid or colonialism as ordained according to eternal law.

Another problematic issue raised in the *Mahābhārata* is this: "Perform actions", "Relinquish them", if both these are Vedic statements, what is the destiny of those who resort to rituals and those who take to knowledge? To this a reply, which has become famous, is given: "A man is bound by action and is liberated by knowledge; so, the far-seeing strivers do not perform action".[141] A little later in the same dialogue this question is asked in a slightly different way: The two sorts of Vedic sentences, viz., "perform" and "relinquish", appear to be contradictory from the empirical standpoint. Are they both valid, or is one of them only valid? The former is not possible, and if the latter, how can a śāstra contain conflicting statements, one valid and another invalid? Without opposing actions, how is liberation possible? To this the answer is: In any life station all those who act as prescribed will reach the supreme stage. One should fulfil one's duties according to the life stations he passes through; whoever is without desire and malice will be glorified in the beyond.[142]

The bewildering varieties of actions, sacraments and rituals prescribed in the Vedas, sūtras and smṛtis and the conflicting statements in each of them and the mutual contradictions among them, gave rise to the first problematic issue mentioned above. The *Māhābhārata* solved it in its various dialogues and, of course, in the *Gītā* too. The second problematic issue arose out of the seeming conflict, especially between the earlier portions of the Veda and its last portion, and it was settled in the *Manusmṛti* and in the different philosophical discourses of the *Mahābhārata* including the *Gītā*. "Which is better, renunciation of actions or yoga of action"? "Both lead to the highest good, but yoga excels". "Indeed, the perpetual renunciant is one who neither hates nor desires; one without the pairs of opposites (nirdvandva) is easily freed from bondage." So run the first three verses of chapter V of the *Gītā*. "I want to know the essence of renunciation (saṁnyāsa) and of relinquishment (tyāga) separately". "Renouncing actions motivated by desire is saṁnyāsa, and relinquishing the fruit of all actions is tyāga". So run the first two verses of the last chapter of the same work. Of course, this kind of answer is suggested in the earlier portions of the Veda also, and quite clearly of all in the first verse of the Īśa Upaniṣad, which is the last chapter of the Śukla Yajurveda-saṁhitā. But the karmakāṇḍa-jñānakāṇḍa harmonisation was probably done clearly and in some detail for the first time by the *Mahābhārata* and the *Manusmṛti*, the nuclei of which were formed not long after the Buddha's age and the earlier versions of which were crystallised by or certainly in the Śuṅga period. Later the Vedāntic systems and the purāṇas made use of this and developed it further.

This is how the smṛti-itihāsa-purāṇas did amplification and supplementation (samupabṛṁhaṇa) of the Veda. The attitude of this literature as well as of the darśanas and the Nirukta towards the Veda is certainly neither one of "sceptical scrutiny", commended by Whitney, nor like "that of an ancient Greek at the oracle of a crazed priestess, or a red Indian at the door of a medicine-lodge", which "amused" or "nauseated" that American Indologist.[143] It is on the whole that of a reasonable* faith.

---

* reasonable = "in accordance with reason; not absurd". (COD 1990)

NOTES

1. There was a recent newspaper report that the Director of the Birla Science Centre, Hyderabad, announced that in his institution studies of Vedic astronomical data and theories led them to propose the date of 7500 B.C. for the Ṛgveda and that it has independent corroborative evidence based on the recent work of two Americans who carbon-dated a copper head as of the 4th millennium. (*The Hindu*, Hyderabad, Friday, August 30, 1991, p. 19). I, for one, remain sceptical.
2. Bk. I, Pt. 1, ch. V, sect. ii, of my *Revelation and Reason in Advaita Vedanta*, reprint, New Delhi, 1974, pp. 75 ff. Details and references are omitted here.
3. Tātparyabhūta mukhyārtha, pradhānabhūta artha.
4. Abhyāsa
5. Ajñātajñāpanam
6. Samyak anvaya. Tātparyam saṁyaktvaṁ.
7. This paragraph and much of the earlier are from the source mentioned in n. 2 above.
8. Tatpratītijananayogyatvam, taditarapratīticchayā-anuccaritatvam. *Vedāntaparibhāṣā.* Pratīti = clear conception or understanding (Macdonell).
9. Ṣaḍliṅga
10. Prakaraṇa
11. Upakrama-parākrama
12. This principle is known as 'apaccheda nyāya'.
13. For detailed exposition of ṣaḍliṅga, upakrama-parākrama and apaccheda-nyāya, see my book, *op. cit.*, pp. 81-87.
14. A.N. Whitehead, cited *op. cit.*, p. 311.
15. *The History and Principles of Vedic Interpretation*, New Delhi, 1983.
16. *op. cit.*, p. 203.
17. "Vyutpattidvāreṇa ca śabdānām parijñānamabhyudayaheturiti śrutirdarśayati". Cited by Ram Gopal.
18. "Abdhirlaṅghita eva vānarabhaṭaiḥ, kiṁtvasya gaṁbhīratāṁ āpātālanimagnapīvaratanuḥ jānāti manthācalaḥ". *Anargharāghava.*
19. Quoted from his *Vedic Religion* by Ram Gopal, *op. cit.*, pp. 203-04.
20. I. 11. 1.
21. See editor's Introduction to Whitney's trans. of *Atharva Veda Saṁhitā*, HOS, Vol. I, pp. xix-xx.
22. This paragraph is based on a booklet of Halle University, Ram Gopal, *op. cit.*, pp. 17, 175 and Valentina Stache-Rosen, *German Indologists*, 2nd rev. edn., by Agnes Stache-Weiske, New Delhi, 1990, pp. 109, 119-20.
23. "Sākṣātkṛtadharmāṇo ṛṣayo babhūvuḥ . . . " *Nirukta*, I. 20.

24. Macdonell.
25. Vātsyāyana, *Nyāya-bhāṣya* I. 1.7; II. 1.69.
26. 'Na pratyakṣam anṛṣeḥ asti mantram'. VIII. 129
27. "Tadyadenāṁstapasyamānān brahma svayaṁbhvabhyānarṣatta ṛṣayo'bhavaṁstadṛṣīṇāmṛṣitvamiti vijñāyate".
28. "Na pṛthaktvena mantrā nirvaktavyāḥ, prakaraṇaśa eva'nirvaktavyāḥ."
29. "Manuṣyā vā ṛṣiṣūtkrāmatsu devānabruvan ko na ṛṣirbhaviṣyatīti. Tebhya etaṁ tarkamṛṣim prāyacchan mantrārthacintābhyūhamabhyūḍham. Tasmādyadeva kiṁcānūcāno 'bhyūhatyārṣam tad bhavati". *Nirukta*, ch. XIII, pariśiṣṭa XII. ed. L. Sarup, p. 227.
30. "Tasmādeteṣu yāvanto'rthā upapadyeran ... sarva eva te yojyāḥ; nātrāparādho'sti". *Ṛjvarthavyākhyā* on the *Nirukta*, II. 8. On the basis of this, in their ṭīkā on the *Nirukta*, VII. 5., Skanda-Maheśvara said, "In all viewpoints all mantras may be applied". Sarvadarśaneṣu sarve mantrā yojanīyāḥ.
31. "Vācaṁ dhenumupāsīta ... Tasyāḥ mano vatsaḥ". *Bṛh. Up.*, V. 8.1.
32. "Vāgiti śabdastrayī tāṁ vācaṁ dhenuṁ ... tasyāḥ ... manovatsaḥ, manaso hi prasrāvyate manasā hyālocite viṣaye vāk pravartate". Bhāṣya on above.
33. Ṛgveda, X. 71. 4-5 already referred to.
34. Yāska, *Nirukta*, I. 19. Apyekaḥ paśyannapaśyati vācam, etc. "Yadvedavākyam ācāryād gṛhītam arthajñānarahitaṁ pāṭharūpeṇa eva punaḥ punaḥ uccāryate, tad kadācidapi ... svārthaṁ na prakāśati... Tathā sati tasya vākyasya vedatvameva mukhyam na syāt, alaukikaṁ puruṣārthopāyam vetti anena iti ...".
35. *A History of Indian Philosophy*, Vol. I, pp. 370, 68.
36. *Pāraskara Gṛhya Sūtra*: Vidhir vidheyas tarkas' ca Vedaḥ.
37. "Samastavaidikatarkopasaṁhārātmikā".
38. "Mīmāṁsāsaṁjñikas tarkaḥ sarva vedasamudbhavaḥ". Quoted in *Nyāyavārttikatātparyaṭīkā*.
39. "Yadetad dvaitasyāsattvamuktam yuktitaḥ tadetad Vedānta-pramāṇāvagatam". Bhāṣya introducing *Kārikā*, II. 31.
40. *Bṛhadāraṇyaka Upaniṣad Bhāṣya*, II. 4.5; IV. 5.6; III. 1.1.
41. *Bhāmatī*, I.1.1. "Vedāntamīmāṁsā tāvat tarka eva".
42. Śaṅkara, *Sūtra-bhāṣya*, and *Ratnaprabhā* on it, I.1.2.
43. *Bhāmatī*, II.1.6. "Āgamapramāṇāśrayaḥ, tadviṣayavivecakaḥ, tadavirodhī".
44. *Siddhāntabindu*, GOS, Baroda, p. 70.
45. "Dharmabrahmaṇī Vedaikavedye". *Puruṣārthānuśāsana*.
46. "Ananyalabhyatvād dharmabrahmaṇorvedaviṣayatvaṁ". Sāyaṇa.
47. Gauḍapāda, *Kārikā*, III. 23.
48. "Puruṣāsvātantryamātram apauruṣeyatvaṁ rocayante Jaiminīyā api taccāsmākam api samānaṁ". Vācaspati, *Bhāmatī*, I.1.3.

49. Śaṅkara, *Bṛhadāraṇyaka-bhāṣya,* Introductory. "Sarvo'pyayaṁ Vedaḥ pratyakṣānumānābhyāmanavagata... prakāśanaparaḥ... Dṛṣṭaviṣaye ... nāgamānveṣaṇā"
50. Same bhāṣya, I.4.10; III.3.1; II.1.20. " ... śāstram ... pravṛttaṁ ... yathābhūtānām ajñātānāṁ jñāpane".
51. *Vedārthasaṅgraha,* 66. " ... padārthagrāhi pratyakṣam; śāstram tu pratyakṣādyaparicchedya ... viṣayam. Iti śāstrapratyakṣayoḥ na virodhaḥ".
52. *Viṣṇu-tattva-vinirṇaya.* "Na ca anubhava-virodhe āgamasya prāmāṇyaṁ".
53. e.g., S. Radhakrishnan, *The Principal Upaniṣads,* p. 49.
54. *Bṛhadāraṇyaka Upaniṣad,* IV.4.22. "Tam etaṁ Vedānuvacanena brāhmaṇā vividiṣanti".
55. *Ṛgveda,* X.82.7. "Nīhāreṇa prāvṛtā jalpyā cā'sutrupa ukthaśāsaścaranti".
56. *Ṛgveda,* X. 71.4, 5, 9. Sāyaṇa-bhāṣya: "Kevalapāṭhako nindyate (5). Vedārthānabhijñā nindyante (9)".
57. Sāyaṇa on the first half of 4 above; and his bhāṣyopakramaṇikā.
58. Same on 5 above; and upakramaṇikā. On this and above, see *Nirukta,* I.19.20.
59. e.g., *Subhāṣitāvali,* 2301, 2303.
60. "Rājamāṣanibhairdantaiḥ kaṭivinyastapāṇayaḥ, dvāri tiṣṭhanti rājendra cchāndasāḥ ślokaśatravaḥ".
61. Ganganatha Jha, *Pūrva Mīmāṁsā in its Sources,* p. 361.
62. For the discussion whether mantras are meaningful, see *Mīmāṁsā Sūtra,* I.2.4. 31 to 53.
63. In *Nyāyaratnākara.* "Nityaniṣiddhayoḥ iṣṭāniṣṭaphalaṁ nāsti".
64. For details and references, see my book *Revelation and Reason in Advaita Vedānta,* New Delhi, 1974, pp. 223-32. For the interesting individual views of Jayanta, a Naiyāyika, ibid., pp.232-36.
65. Mahābhāsya: "Rakṣohāgamalaghvasamdehāḥ prayojanaṁ". (Āgama here is prayojaka but not prayojana, as indicated by Patañjali himself and explained by Kaiyaṭa.)
66. Based on *Sāṁkhya* Sūtra. For references see source mentioned in n. 64, pp. 221-22.
67. *Kārikā* 2, with Gauḍapāda's bhāṣya.
68. This account is almost wholly based on *Yogasūtrabhāṣya.* For references, see source mentioned in n. 64, pp. 220-21.
69. This account is completely based on Kaṇāda and Praśastapāda only. For references, *op. cit.,* pp.222-23.
70. *Manusmṛti,* II. 2-5. "Kāmātmatā na praśastā ... " to "sarvān kāmān samaśnute".
71. Ibid., XII. 82-92. "Eṣa sarvaḥ samuddiṣṭaḥ ... " to "Vedābhyāse ca yatnavān".

72. The *Mahābhārata*, critical edn., Poona, 1971, Vol. I, pp. 665, 668, 669. The sentence in square brackets occurs in some recensions, not in the critical edn.
73. *op. cit.*, 1972, Vol. II, p. 948.
74. *op. cit.*, p. 949. "Satye sthito yastu sa vedavedyaṁ".
75. Ibid., "Ya eva satyānnāpaiti sa jñeyo brāhmaṇaḥ".
76. For Syūmaraśmi's statements, *op. cit.*, 1974, Vol. III, pp. 2338-41: e.g. "Yo brāhmaṇo yajate vedaśāstraiḥ, ūrdhvaṁ yajñaḥ paśubhiḥ sārthameti". "Nāyaṁ loka'styayajñānāṁ paraśceti viniścayaḥ". "Aśraddadhānairaprājñaiḥ ... nirāśairalasaiḥ śrāntaiḥ ... śramasyoparamo dṛṣṭaḥ pravrajyā nāma paṇḍitaiḥ". "Nāstikyamanyathā ca syādvedānām pṛṣṭhataḥ kriyā".
77. "Apavarge'tha saṁtyāge buddhau ca kṛtaniścayāḥ".
78. "Brahmiṣṭhāḥ brahmabhūtāśca brahmaṇyeva kṛtālayāḥ".
79. "Teṣām . . . gārhasthye kiṁ prayojanam?"
80. Taking 'dhī' to mean 'devotion' and 'yajña' to mean 'worship', verse 19 in XII. 261 of the epic has been translated thus. 'Dhī' means 'devotion', 'prayer' also; and 'yajña' means 'worship' also. (A.A. Macdonell, *A Practical Sanskrit Dictionary*)
81. This implies that his whole life itself is askesis and sacrifice. "Dvārāṇi yasya sarvāṇi suguptāni manīṣiṇaḥ, upasthamudaraṁ bāhū vākcaturthī sa vai dvijaḥ. Moghānyaguptadvārasya sarvāṇyeva bhavantyuta, kiṁ tasya tapasā kāryaṁ kiṁ yajñena kimātmanā".
82. "Sudurjñeyāḥ jñātāścāpi duṣkarāḥ, anuṣṭhitāścāntavantaḥ".
83. śāstradasyavaḥ, brahmastenāḥ.
84. "Apavargagatirnityo yatidharmaḥ sanātanaḥ, sādhāraṇaḥ kevalo vā yathābalamupāsyate".
85. "Nirāpaddharma ācārastvapramādo'parābhavaḥ, sarvavarṇeṣu yatteṣu nāsītkaścidvyatikramaḥ".
86. Ānṛśaṁsyaṁ kṣamā śāntirahiṁsā satyamārjavam, adroho nābhimānaśca hrīstitikṣā śamastathā. Panthāno brahmaṇastvete".
87. gas (slang) = pointless idle talk. (COD, 1990). Vātareṭakaḥ = one who emits 'gas'.
88. For this entire account of Kapila's discourse, see *Mahābhārata* crit. edn., Vol. III, Poona, 1974, pp. 2237-42.
89. The Manubṛhaspati dialogue is more forceful in its disparagement of action. Action, it says, is of the nature of guṇas; it is for one who aspires only for happiness and not for the supreme Brahman, which is outside the path of action. "paraṁ hi tatkarmapathādapetaṁ". It in fact states: That from which all this world has been generated and on which the words of (Vedic) mantras have not shed light is the Immutable. "Yato jagatsarvamidaṁ prasūtaṁ . . . yanmantraśabdairakṛtaprakāśaṁ . . . tadakṣaraṁ . . . ". *op. cit.*, pp. 2255-56.

90. This is dvaya-mantra: "I take refuge at the two feet of Nārāyaṇa who has Śrī"; "I bow down to Nārāyaṇa who is always with Śrī". "Śrīmannārāyaṇacaraṇau śaraṇam prapadye; Śrīmate Nārāyaṇāya namaḥ".
91. 'prāpya-prāpaka', 'upāyopeya', 'upāyavaraṇa' and 'ātmasamarpaṇa'.
92. *Śrīmad Vālmīki Rāmāyaṇa*, 2nd edn., ed. T.R. Krishnacharya, Vol. I, Kumbakonam, 1929, 'Ayodhyākāṇḍa', 109. 10-14. "Satye lokaḥ pratiṣṭhitaḥ. Dharmaḥ satyaṁ paro loke. Satyameveśvaro loke. Satyamūlāni sarvāṇi satyānnāsti paraṁ padam. Vedāḥ satyapratiṣṭhānāstasmātsatyaparo bhavet".
93. *Ibid.*, Vol. II, 1930, 'Yuddhakāṇḍa', 120.12ff. The translation of the quoted Sanskrit sentences is in accordance with the traditional interpretation. But, instead of "the Vedas are your breath", it may be translated as "the Vedas are your instructions", for'Saṁskāra' has also the meanings of 'training, education". (Macdonell's *A Practical Sanskrit Dictionary.*)
94. *Śrimad Bhāgavata*, VI.2.24: "Dharmaṁ bhāgavataṁ śuddhaṁ traividyaṁ ca guṇāśrayaṁ". I have chosen to use the term 'God' for 'Bhagavān'.
95. *op. cit.*, VI.3.22-25: "Etāvāneva loke'smin puṁsāṁ dharmaḥ paraḥ smṛtaḥ, bhaktiyogo bhagavati tannāmagrahaṇādibhiḥ. Etāvatālamaghanirharaṇāya puṁsāṁ, saṁkīrtanaṁ bhagavato guṇakarmanāmnāṁ; .... Prāyeṇa veda tadidaṁ na mahājano'yaṁ, devyā vimohitamatirbata māyayālaṁ; trayyāṁ jaḍīkṛtamatirmadhupuṣpitāyām, vaitānike mahati karmaṇi yujyamānaḥ".
96. *op.cit.*, X.87.3. "Saiṣā hyupaniṣadbrāhmī . . . ".
97. *op.cit.*, X.87.36. "Bhramayati bhāratī ta uruvṛttibhirukthajaḍān".
98. *op.cit.*, X.87.50. "Yo'syotprekṣaka ādimadhyanidhane ... taṁ kaivalyanirastayonimabhayaṁ dhyāyedajasraṁ hariṁ".
99. *op.cit.*, XI.18.30. "Vedavādarato na syānna pāṣaṁḍī na haitukaḥ . . .".
100. "Idam Gītāśāstraṁ samastavedārthasārasaṅgrahabhūtaṁ durvijñeyaṁ".
101. *Bhagavadgītā*, II. 41-46. In this context I have chosen to translate "buddhi' as 'thinking'. In their word-for-word translation, Annie Besant and Bhagavan Das translated it as 'thought'; and in their translations of these verses F. Edgerton as 'mental attitude' and J.A.B. van Buitenen as 'spirit'. R.C. Zaehner preceded van Buitenen in doing so.
102. Śaṅkara's bhāṣya on the *Gītā*, II. 46. This śruti text is from *Chāndogyopaniṣad*, IV.1.4. "Sarvaṁ tadabhisameti yatkiñca prājaḥ sādhu kurvanti yastadveda yat sa veda". The *Gītā* text is IV.33: "Sarvaṁ karmā'khilaṁ pārtha jñāne parisamāpyate".
103. Rāmānuja's bhāṣya on the *Gītā*, II. 46. "Yathā udapāne pipāsoḥ yāvad eva prayojanaṁ pānīyaṁ tāvad eva tena upādīyate na sarvam. Evaṁ

sarveṣu Vedeṣu . . . vaidikasya mumukṣoḥ yadeva mokṣasādhanaṁ tadeva upādeyaṁ . . . na anyat".

104. *Gītā*, II. 52-53.
105. Bhāṣya on *ibid.*
106. *Gītā*, XVI. 23-24.
107. *op.cit.*, XV. 20.
108. *Brahma-sūtra*, I.2.6.
109. *op.cit.*, IV.3.11.
110. *Gītā*, II. 49.
111. *op.cit.*, XVIII. 63.
112. *op.cit.*, IX. 20-21. gatāgataṁ gamanāgamanaṁ . . . na tu svātantrayaṁ . . . (Śaṅkara).
113. *op.cit.*, XVIII. 5-6.
114. *op.cit.*, IV. 32.
115. *op.cit.*, III. 9.
116. *op.cit.*, VIII. 11, 28. The Imperishable is supreme Brahman, while the same embodied is the individual soul. Śaṅkara's bhāṣya on VIII. 2.
117. *op.cit.*, XI. 47-48, 54.
118. *op.cit.*, XIII.4. My translation follows Śaṅkara's bhāṣya. He explained 'chandobhiḥ' as 'chandāṁsi ṛgādīni taiḥ chandobhiḥ', 'pṛthak' as 'vivekataḥ', and 'brahmasūtrapadaiḥ' as 'brahmaṇaḥ sūcakāni vākyāni . . . taiḥ padyate gamyate jñāyate brahma iti tāni padāni ucyante'. As an example of such a sentence he gave, "The Self alone is to be meditated upon (Ātmetyevopāsīta)". (*Bṛhadāraṇyaka*, I.4.7.) The word 'padanīyaṁ' in the sense of 'knowable' occurs in that Upaniṣadic passage.
119. *op.cit.*, XV.1. My translation follows Śaṅkara's bhāṣya; Portions in brackets are from it.
120. *op.cit.*, XV. 15. Both F. Edgerton and J.A.B. van Buitenen think that in "Vedāntakṛt" (maker of Vedānta), Vedānta certainly means the Upaniṣads. Śaṅkara takes it to mean 'the maker of the tradition of the meaning of Vedānta', and thus preserves the apauruṣeyatā (impersonality) of the Upaniṣads. The Advaitins believe the primal guru of Advaita was Nārāyaṇa.
121. *op.cit.*, XV.18.
122. *op.cit.*, XVII.23-28.
123. 'anṛtavyāghātapunarukta' doṣas. *Nyāyasūtra*, II.1.57-68.
124. 'ātmasaṁskāra' and 'yoga'. *op.cit.*, IV.2. 38, 46.
125. *op.cit.*, sūtra 47.
126. "Tattvādhyavasāyasaṁrakṣaṇārthaṁ". *op.cit.*, IV.2.50.
127. Louis Renou, *The Destiny of the Veda in India*, Delhi, 1965, p. 53.
128. *Manusmṛti*, XII. 105-06.
129. *Ibid.*, IV. 176.
130. Yājñavalkyasmṛti, VI. 156.

131. Cited by Surama Dasgupta. *Development of Moral Philosophy in India*, Calcutta, 1961, p. 23.
132. *Mahābhārata*, crit. edn., Vol. III, p. 2183. ". . . dharmādharmaviniścaye buddhimāsthāya . . . vartitavyam".
133. "Viśvāmitraśvapacasaṁvāda", p.2179, verses 1 to 8.
134. *Gītā*, II. 49.
135. *Manusmṛti*, II.6.
136. *op.cit.*, II.12.
137. *op.cit.*, II.13.
138. *op.cit.*, II.1.
139. *Mahābhārata*, crit. edn., Vol. III, p. 2326, ślokas 7 to 10 in XII. 252 in yudhiṣṭhira's questions leading to the narration of Tulādhāra-Jājalisaṁvāda.
140. *op.cit.*, p.2328. "Adroheṇaiva bhūtānāmalpadroheṇa vā punaḥ, yā vṛttiḥ sa paro dharmaḥ . . . ".
141. *Ibid.*, p. 2308. "Karmaṇā badhyate janturvidyayā tu pramucyate . . . ". This is from "Śukānupraśna".
142. *Ibid.*, p. 2309. "Akāmadveṣasaṁyuktaḥ sa paratra mahīyate".
143. "American Journal of Philology", Vol. VII, cited by G.A. Jacob, *A Concordance to the Principal Upaniṣads and the Bhagavadgīta*, Reprint, Delhi, 1985, Preface, p.6.

CHAPTER THREE

Unity and Essence of the Veda

I

Harmonising the Vedas

In the earliest time there was only one Veda, the sacred syllable OṀ was speech in its entirety, there was only God Nārāyaṇa and nothing else, there was only one fire and one caste: so declares the *Śrīmadbhāgavata*.[1] This work and the *Mahābhārata* inform us that Satyavatī's son* divided, classified and edited the one Vedic 'tree' into branches; and so came to be known as Vyāsa.[2] This happens in every aeon. If there is any truth in this Aitihāsic-Purāṇic account, by reflecting on the four Vedas as they are constituted now, the rationale of the division of the one Veda appears to be as follows: (1) Most of the sūktas concerned with ontology have gone to make up the *Ṛgveda*. Ṛks are those which laud or describe absolute Being: ṛcanti stuvanti varṇayanti vā sattattvaṁ iti ṛcaḥ. They constitute the first Veda; they impart ontological knowledge. (2) If supreme knowledge is the subject of the first Veda, that of the second is supreme action. Yajña (sacrifice) is the supreme action, says the great brāhmaṇa attached to the Kāṇva recension of this Veda.[3] 'Yajus' or 'Adhvara' is sacrifice, which is the best action, as it purifies the mind, and the Veda which shows how to perform it in the proper way is *Yajurveda*. (3) As the *Chāndogya Upaniṣad* said, what is ṛk is sāman.[4] What is

---

* and, of course, Parāśara's.

lauded or described through the former is chanted or meditated through the latter. Sāmans are conciliatory words, or chants. They make up the *Sāmaveda.* (4) The *Atharva Veda,* according to Sāyaṇa, contains the essence of all the Vedas and so is superior.[5] It propounds the Brahman-Ātman identity and the duties of 'Brahmā',[6] one of the four officiating priests in sacrifices.* As a 'Brahmā' named Atharvā 'saw' the fourth Veda, it is called after him.[7]

It is not correct to think that the *Atharva* is not a part of the Vedic canon and that only the other three** constitute it. The *Ṛgveda* itself and the *Yajurveda* state that the sage who generated fire by attrition and promulgated the sacrificial path was Atharvā.[8] Atharvā and his progeny received and transmitted the revelation contained in this Veda, so it came to be known as the *Atharva Veda.* The Bhṛgus also shared this privilege with them. The gotra of both was Āṅgirasa. So, sometimes it is referred to as *Atharvāṅgirasa* Veda, *Bhṛgvaṅgirasa* Veda, and even just as *Āṅgiro Veda* in this Veda itself and in the *Gopatha* and *Śatapatha* Brāhmaṇas respectively. The *Chāndogya,* the *Bṛhadāraṇyaka* and the *Taittirīya Upaniṣads* refer to this fourth Veda as the *Atharvāṅgirasa Veda,* while the *Muṇḍaka Upaniṣad* names it as *Atharva Veda.*[9] According to both Yāska and Patañjali, in the Ṛgvedic mantra which is understood to conceive the Word-Absolute as a bull having four horns, by the latter are meant the four Vedas.[10] Thus the Brāhmaṇas and the oldest Upaniṣads and also Yāska and Patañjali as well as the earliest stratum of the *Mahābhārata**** accepted the Vedas to be four; and Atharva is known to the *Ṛgveda* and *Yajurveda.* Its religious and philosophical importance is no whit less than that of any other Veda.

---

* The other three are Hotā, Adhvaryu and Udgātā; their duties are respectively known from the Ṛg, Yajur and Sāma Vedas.

** The word *trayī,* it is explained by some, only signifies the three kinds of mantras in the Veda: Vedagatamantratraividhyanidānatvāt.

*** e.g.,"Śukānupraśna" (crit. edn., Vol. III, p.2301).

(1) The main purpose of the *Ṛgveda* from its first to its last manḍala is to impart the knowledge of the *One Real* (ekam sat) spoken of and imagined variously; "Ekam sadviprā bahudhā vadanti. Viprāḥ kavayo vacobhirekaṁ santaṁ bahudhā kalpayanti".[11] "Then that one (Tadekam) alone was without any other"[12]. "Those who do not know That, what, will they do with the ṛks?" asks this Veda; and replies, " but those who know That firmly abide in their own nature (i.e., are liberated).[13] (2) The *Śukla Yajurveda* begins with an invocation to God to rouse one for undertaking the best action for full advancement of oneself, describes the sacrificial path, while constantly reminding that only by knowing the Great person one transcends mortality and that there is no other path for that, and concludes with the affirmation of : (a) everything being encompassed by the Lord, and (b) one's duty to enjoy through relinquishing: Tena tyaktena bhuñjīthāḥ.[14] (3) The *Sāmaveda* is mentioned by the *Bhagavadgītā* to be the divine 'power manifestation' (vibhūti) among the Vedas. The *Chāndogya Upaniṣad* calls it the flower of the Vedic tree.[15] Being a collection of ṛks, it is based on the *Ṛgveda.*[16] In fact, "Sāma" means that in which *amaḥ* (*svara,* musical note) connected with *sā* (=*ṛk*) exists: 'Sā ca amaśceti tatsāmnaḥ sāmatvaṁ.' So the speciality of *Sāmaveda* is that it consists of mantras which can be sung, while the other three Vedas consist of mantras only. Not mere mantras or mere songs, but mantras which can be sung are called Sāmans, according to Jaimini: Gītiṣu sāmākhyā.[17] Svara is the condition or state of sāmans;[18] it is their intrinsic nature.[19] In the Ṛg, Yajur and Atharva Vedas there is a good deal of praise of Sāmans. The gods protect the person versed in *Sāmaveda* and in its chanting; the 'pure deity' is to be prayed to through 'pure Sāma';[20] Ṛks and Sāmans are the dear abodes of Brahman.[21] The Ṛgvedic affirmative assertions of Being appear transformed into rhapsodic songs in the *Sāmaveda.* (4) The main purpose of the *Atharva Veda*

is to reveal the Brahman in man (ye puruṣe brahma viduḥ), the indwelling marvellous spiritual entity known to Brahman-knowers (yakṣamātmanvattadvai brahmavido viduḥ).[22] According to Śaṅkarācārya, in the mantras of this Veda actions which stabilise peace, prosperity, etc., have importance.[23]

Thus all the Vedas may be considered to have a unity of purport and singleness of ultimate concern , which comes to light through a harmonic (samanvayic*) understanding of them. The greatest known interpreter of the Vedas, Sāyaṇa has asserted: "Through all the Vedas it is, indeed, Brahman that is ascertained . This is well-known in the case of their Upaniṣadic portions; even in the case of their other portions which have sacrifice, etc., as their subject, as through purification of mind they become the means of knowing Brahman, the latter (i.e., Brahman) becomes their subject."[24] Ātmānanda asserts this with greater force: "The entire Veda is concerned with Brahman." "The Vedic portion dealing with ritual has the meaning of the word THOU for its subject. The portion dealing with the Lord having attributes (saguṇeśa) has the meaning of the word THAT as its subject. The Vedāntic portion is, obviously, devoted to the oneness of Brahman and Ātman. Thus, all the Vedas have as their subject the oneness of Brahman and Ātman.[25]

Both Sāyaṇa and Ātmānanda, as followers of Advaita Vēdānta, echo the view of Śaṅkarācārya and his disciples. Explaining the *Kaṭha* Upaniṣadic passage which speaks of the goal to be attained proclaimed by all the Vedas, Śaṅkara adds that they do so 'without any discord'.[26] In the *Bṛhadāraṇyaka Bhāṣya,* Śaṅkara says that the Veda consists of two parts, that which lays down injunctions and prohi-

* samanvaya=samyak-anvaya, proper mutual connection of the different parts of a book or of different books of a corpus. This is achieved by an application of six criteria which go to help in determining the tātparya of a work or a collection of works. The Mīmāṁsā has described and illustrated them.

bitions and the other made up by the Upaniṣads; and remarks that those who are exclusively involved in the former, which propounds only what exists for nescience, enter into darkness.[27] Elsewhere in the same bhāṣya he affirms that the entire Veda is useful in the case of Ātman, as the Upaniṣad itself inclusively states so comprehending the whole Veda, because the whole complex of obligatory daily actions, performed without desire, through generation of self-knowledge, become the means of liberation. Thus there is, according to him, mutual coherence between the Vedic portion dealing with actions and that dealing with knowledge.[28]

There is no difference among the great ācāryas regarding the whole of the Veda having consistency and unity of purport, though they differ as to what that purport is. Thus, Rāmānujācārya holds that the Vedas teach the nature of Nārāyaṇa, who is the Supreme Brahman, and the mode of his worship.[29] Similarly, Madhvācārya cites several texts from itihāsa-purāṇas to establish that throughout the Veda it is Viṣṇu who is sung, that all the Vedas are concerned with Him and depend upon him.[30] On the other hand, Haradattaśivācārya, on whose work Śrīkaṇṭhācārya and Appayya Dīkṣita rely, declares that all the sentences in the Vedas, as well as those in the tantras in accordance with the former, propound only Śiva as the supreme reality. The mass of words known as the Veda, he says, is severally divided into mantras, arthavādas and vidhis, and is an independent source of knowledge. Yet, Haradatta adds, when its words and their meanings are critically examined by the impartial, it is found to reveal Śiva alone as the Lord.[31] This shows that all who accepted the authority of the Veda were certain that its import is one and only one; but there is no unanimity among them whether it is the Absolute, the Supreme Person, or Moral Law.

It may be inserted here that even according to some Western authorities, e.g., Maurice Bloomfield, in view of the position of the Upaniṣads in the śrauta (scriptural) texts as well as in "a higher sense" they are indeed Vedānta, "End of the Veda", "the texts of the Veda's highest religion and philosophy".[32] Louis Renou too found no opposition between the earlier portions of the Veda and the Upaniṣads, as the latter supplement the former, carrying forward the speculations of the hymns and the Brāhmaṇas: "The aim of the whole thought may be expressed as the attempt to formulate the Upaniṣads."[33] Another scholar, Lüders commented: "To have made truth the highest principle of life, that is a deed for which people, even modern peoples, might envy those ancients". (*Varuṇa*, Göttingen, 1951,1959).* In the last sentence, by the word "ancients" Lüders meant the "Āryans" only. However, the correct position according to later and deeper research has been set forth thus by F.R. Allchin and Bridget Allchin:" The Ṛgveda is the result of cooperation between the Āryans and non-Āryans".

To resume what has been said earlier, the contentions of the great Mīmāṁsakas and of the great Vedāntins mentioned above, regarding the meaning of the Veda are reasonable.

Kumārila and Prabhākara did not reject the validity and authority of the Upaniṣads. They expressly stated that: (1) they were against the denial of the self; (2) the detailed knowledge of the self could be got from Vedānta-niṣevaṇa (Vedāntic practice) only; (3) it is not at all necessary to perform the rituals for fulfilment of desires mentioned in the Veda unless one desires such fulfilment through them: (4) performance of obligatory regular duties without desires is necessary for getting rid of passions (kaṣāya), and moreover, that too with a sense of dedication of the fruits of such actions to God, for attaining the ultimate good; and, lastly, (5) moral knowledge, including what are duties and what are not, can be obtained only from the Veda.[34]

* But, cp. Paul Thieme who thought Vedic poetry is "Zweek-Dichtung".

The minimum on which there is unanimity among all Vedāntins may be indicated thus: the World-cause and World-ground (Brahman) is One and is conscious (cetana); the complete indirect (parokṣa) knowledge of That One can be got only from śruti and not at all through empirical means. Their principal difference may be said to be on this point: according to some, Brahman is of the nature of consciousness and bliss (Vijñāna and ānanda), and it has neither attributes or qualities (guṇas) nor anything besides itself; but according to others Brahman is a Person who has infinite auspicious (kalyāṇa) guṇas including the two principal ones, viz., vijñāna and ānanda, is transcendent as well as immanent and all encompassing, with everything being either a mode of Him or dependent on Him. While the former hold that pure knowledge of Brahman leads to liberation, the latter assert knowledge transformed into loving devotion (bhakti) of Him leads to it. For all of them śruti is the final and supreme authority.

All that has been maintained in this section was summed up long ago by some Vedic texts themselves: "Where all the Vedas become one". Sarve Vedā yatraikaṁ bhavanti. (*Taittirīya Āraṇyaka*, III.11.) This means, as Rāmānujācārya explained, as the One only is what is spoken of by all the Vedas, they are unanimous. (*Vedārthasaṁgraha*) The *Kaṭha Upaniṣad* (II. 95.) also declared that all the Vedas reveal only one Goal. Sarve Vedā yatpadamāmananti.

II
THE VEDA AND EMPIRICAL KNOWLEDGE

Risking repetition I would like to emphasize again the classical position that the Veda is only that which makes known what is unknown through other sources of knowledge and also not contradicted by them (pramāṇāntarānadhigatābādhita; ajñātajñāpaka). That which makes known dharma and Brahman is the Veda. Yo dharma brahma ca vedayati sa Veda iti Vedalakṣaṇaṁ. The

Mīmāṁsakas, who do not accept creation and dissolution of the world, describe the Vedic tradition as beginningless and continuous, as no author of it is remembered (karturasmaraṇa). So, it is 'impersonal'. The Vedāntins accept creation and dissolution, and Brahman or the Supreme Self as source of the Veda, but do not accept that Brahman had any freedom in its composition. In the sense that it never had a free author, it is 'impersonal' (puruṣāsvātantryalakṣanaṁ apauruṣeyatvam). If any modern Hindu scholar or religious person has thought and said something different about the Veda, he should have made it clear that it is not that of the classical Mīmāṁsā or Vedānta.

While I myself find it difficult to accept the apauruṣeyatva of the Veda as defined by these two schools, I accept Brahman's śāstrayonitva (being the source) of *any* holy scripture; and I do consider the Veda to be one such *par excellence*. The *Śvetāśvatara* Upaniṣad-*Bhagavadgītā* position that He 'delivers' the Vedas (Vedāṁśca prahiṇoti) and is the author of Vedānta (Vedāntakṛt) and verily the One to be known from all the Vedas, satisfies me; and so does the definition of the Veda as what makes known Dharma and Brahman.

Consequently, I am sceptical about the attempts to discover empirical knowledge in the Veda and to glorify it for being a repository of it*. It undoubtedly contains some protoscience and a number of valuable mathematical and scientific ideas , insights and facts, as well as historical data. But the " Vedahood of the Veda", as the *Manusmṛti* pointed out, consists in this: through it is known the means (upāya) which is not apprehended by perception or inference.[35] To have so conceived a holy scripture is one of the greatest achievements of Indian epistemology. Sacred knowledge

* The Upavedas (e.g., Āyur- and Dhanur-vedas) and Vedāṅgas (e.g., Śikṣā, Vyākaraṇa) obviously contain empirical knowledge.

(pavitra jñāna, Gītā, IV. 38) and secular knowledge cannot be mutually replicative.

Pāṇini's work may throw some light on India of his time, and from Kālidāsa's works we may glean something about the society of his time. The works of Caraka and Varāhamihira do contain some metaphysics and ethics while assiduous scanning of Śaṅkara's bhāṣyas showed that in his time there was no universal sovereign in the country, while, perhaps, much ritualism and superstition prevailed. But the essence, uniqueness and greatness of their works is not because of these. Similarly, to desire to obtain empirical knowledge from the Veda is like "the desire to get a piece of cloth enough to cover the pudendum from the kalpadruma", the tree which yields all wishes.[36] The Veda has far more valuable knowledge to convey. Among other things, the *Bṛhadāraṇyaka Upaniṣad* informs that "he who wishes to have a long-living son who would learn all the Vedas, be a great scholar and a sweet-speaking victorious debater in learned assemblies, should have rice cooked with the meat of a vigorous bull, and he and his wife should eat it with clarified butter".[37] Maybe doing so exactly in the way prescribed in the text would give or not give the desired result. But I consider this Upaniṣad to be a holy scripture, one of the greatest spiritual texts and one of the most profound philosophical works, not for its contents like this, but for the illuminating and emancipating truth it gives regarding Brahman. An assessment of this sort is applicable *mutatis mutandis* not only to the entire Veda, but to all scriptures.

III
Yajña

The Vedic is commonly known as a sacrificial religion. It is indeed so though not in a pejorative sense at all. When the essential meaning of sacrifice (yajña), as found in the appropriate passages in the Vedic corpus, especially in the later texts, is grasped, it would be realised that all action not performed for the sake of sacrifice 'binds'. (*Gītā*, III.9.)

Saṁhitās

The Saṁhitās contain somewhat different doctrines about sacrifice, though they could all be reconciled by distinguishing between the higher spiritual and lower religious viewpoints.

Sacrifice is an act of worship, a sign of subjection and honour to a tremendous numinous power one confronts, the external action being only a symbol of this submission. Sacrifice may also be a result of the belief that man is dependent on God, that it is from Him that all things are received, and that unless this fact is acknowledged both inwardly and in an external act, when something given by God Himself is offered to him, one is not truthful to facts (in tune with *ṛta*) and God is not also pleased till then.

Since the Vedic people knew that their existence and well-being depended upon God, this only means that man's prayers and worship bless and glorify God. Men are created to worship and sacrifice, while God exists from eternity, upholds the cosmic order, takes care of all beings, governing them and rewarding and punishing them in accordance with ṛta. Thus in a way the world is God's offering to beings, it is his sacrifice. He creates it to enable us all to exist and enjoy.[38]

The Vedic people mostly thought of sacrifices as acts of pleasing the Deity, the means for getting the favour of God—welfare and material prosperity—along the path of *ṛta*.[39] They were gift offerings for favours without any consciousness of sin.

A sacrificer must be an upholder of truth (*satyadhṛt*); sacrifices are a binding force between men and gods;[40] they are for the good of all,[41] hence a social duty.[41(a)] Not to sacrifice is, therefore, a social calamity, an inhuman thing. Hymns, oblations, fire [42]—praise and laudation of the deity, offering something to him to express one's submission and veneration, and destroyal of this gift by casting it into fire—such is the essence of Vedic sacrifice.

There is, however, an important exception. In the Puruṣa Sūkta,[43] after saying that Puruṣa (the Person) is all this as well as what has been and shall be, and that one-fourth of him is all the creatures, three-fourths of him is eternal life, it is said the gods sacrificed with Puruṣa as the oblation. His limbs were torn and scattered. From that all came, for Puruṣa divided is everything. Gods sacrificing sacrificed the Puruṣa (yajñena yajñaṁ ayajanta devāḥ); these were the first *dharmas*; by them did the mighty ones gain heaven. It is difficult to understand what the hymn means. Sāyaṇa says the gods performed this sacrifice mentally with Puruṣa as the victim. This means that they meditated upon the whole world as being made from the body of the great Puruṣa. If everything is Puruṣa, anything sacrificed becomes the Puruṣa.

Interpreting this verse on the analogy of a somewhat similar verse in the *Gītā* (IV.24), it may be understood to say that as everything depends upon Puruṣa for its existence who is also their end, all is Puruṣa—whether the oblation, the fire, or the sacrificer. Everything belongs to Puruṣa, the one Supreme Being, and is an effect of him; so in offering anything we offer to him what is his own. Puruṣa ensouls everything, so he is everything (*puruṣātmakaṁ sarvam*). Creation is God's sacrifice for he brings forth out of himself all beings and offers them what is his for their enjoyment. He is the source of all things and their support. So meditated the world becomes a way to win the vision of God, and a communion because it consciously unites all beings by an inalienable bond, for they all live in him and on him, fed by him.

Brāhmaṇas and Āryaṇyakas

We may sum up the teaching of the *Brāhmaṇas* in the

following way. Prajāpati, the primal person, was the original sacrificer who sacrificed himself, and thus regained himself. Sacrifice is a universal principle of life.[44] It lives on all creatures, and by it are creatures perpetuated.[45] What is offered is the life of gods, men and fathers. He who voluntarily offers becomes immortal. The gods owe their immortality to sacrifice.[46] In sacrifice man imitates gods and adopts their habits.[47] Sacrifice is commensurate with man and the true sacrifice is that of oneself.[48] Man is reborn by consecration, for his old being is burnt up as an offering to gods, and he gains a new divine life.[49] The oblations of horses, sheep and rice are only meant to be substitutes, symbols of self-giving.[50] By sacrifice one escapes death in the other life one has to live after the death on earth; for in the other world one has to repeatedly die till immortality is gained. Sacrifice confers immortality by making man born into an eternal life. The highest type of sacrifice is meditation on the Supreme Being and realization of one's own nature.

Although the *Brāhmaṇas* speak of a bewildering variety of rituals and gods, they emphatically assert that the Supreme Self is the one that is worshipped by different names in different ways. He unites all (*eṣaḥ hi idaṁ sarvaṁ yunakti*), in him all is the same (*etasmin hi idaṁ sarvaṁ* samānam), for he only gives rise to everything (*eṣaḥ hi idaṁ sarvaṁ utthāpayati*). As whatever object he is worshipped, he becomes that, and protects (or saves) the worshippers accordingly. He assumes the forms men need and becomes accessible in whatsoever way that suits them.* (*Tam yathā upāsate, tadeva bhavati—avati*).[51] That One only is called Brahman in all beings, as the *Taittirīya Āraṇyaka* says[52] (*Sarveṣu bhūteṣu tameva brahmetyācakṣate*). Offering of oneself to Brahman is sacrifice, that is the gist and the sumtotal of *Brāhmaṇa* Wisdom.

---

* It has not been noticed by the commentators that in language and thought as well the *Gītā* (IV. II) echoes this Brāhmaṇa.

In the *Brāhmaṇaṣ* and *Āraṇyakas,* we also find another beautiful conception which transforms sacrifice into acts of mercy. There are five sacrifices, they say, which a man must continuously perform throughout his life, which are not only great sacrifices, but great sacrificial sessions (*sattras*).[53] That which is performed for the good of oneself only is just a sacrifice, whereas that which is performed for the good of all beings and for one's enlightenment is a great sacrifice, a great *sattra.*[54] In this sense sacrifice ceases to be a ritual, and becomes as Bharadvāja said, skill in action. *Yajñaḥ karmasu* kauśalam. *The Gītā* later adopted this by substituting Yogaḥ for Yajñaḥ.[55]

These five great sacrifices are 'brahmayajña', 'devayajña', 'pitṛyajña', 'manuṣyayajña' and 'bhūtayajña'. Brahmayajña is sacrifice to Brahman, the study and teaching of the Veda. The texts studied are the oblations offered to Brahman and the results of scriptural study are mental concentration and peace, control of the senses, steadfastness, growth in spiritual insight and fame. Scriptural study makes one a physician of souls, who can perfect the people. *Paramacikitsaka ātmano bhavati. Prajñāvṛddhiḥ; yaśolokapaktiḥ.*[56] The spiritual truths in the scriptures must be studied and known, and taught to all those who want them, for to do otherwise would be to close for oneself the doors to God.[57] Worship of God and offering to him what one has, symbolized by the Vedic daily sacrificial rituals, is devyajña, sacrifice to God. Holding one's progenitors and ancestors with reverence and gratitude in one's memory, daily prayers for their welfare in the other world and offerings in honour of them, is pitṛyajña, the sacrifice for the ancestors. To offer what one has to the needy and the poor who approach one, to go to the succour of one's fellows, service of man—this is manuṣyayajña, sacrifice to men. He who cooks for himself, says Manu, eats sin.[58] What we earn and cook must be for the sake of anyone who needs and approaches us for help. Care of animals and birds, in short all non-human beings, and offering of food for them is bhūtayajña, sacrifice for beings. Maintenance and furthering of all life is bhūtayajña. This is symbolized in the compulsory daily offering of food to dogs, crows and pariahs.[59] Man is indebted to gods, ancestors and sages, for the first two are responsible for his existence and well-being, while it is the writings of sages which awaken him to his situation and enable him to work for his salvation. He discharges these debts by performing these sacrifices to them. All life is one, all men and living beings are kin; so it is every man's duty to do what he can to serve them by caring for them and by sharing with them what he has.

Moreover, everyone's life is a struggle for existence, one injures the interests of others constantly by one's own actions and speech knowingly or unknowingly. Everyone lives to some extent on others' toil and life, and the very content, preparation and eating of our food is achieved by the knowing and unknowing slaughter of countless animals, organisms and plant life.[60] Redemption from all this sin is secured by sharing with other men and beings what one has, by performing manuṣya and bhūta yajñas. True sacrifice is mercy, compassion, bhūtadayā, not only for men, but for all beings, the experience of kinship with all life, and the action that is motivated by this feeling. Only by living for others can one redeem oneself from sin; to toil and struggle, cook and eat merely for oneself is sinful.[61]

Implicit in the conception of the five mahāyajñas as the means of redemption for man is the assumption that man is in spiritual and physical union with all existence; he is a part of the cosmos, he is related to infinite Being. A philosophy which only concerns itself with man and society is blind to this truth, and, on the other hand, a mysticism which emphasizes only man's relationship with the transcendent eternal Being ignores what is all around us and denies significance to action. Man stands in relation not only to the transcendent and the eternal, but also to the existent and the finite; he is related to all being, all existence. To recognise this unity and interdependence of all existence and especially of all life, and to manifest this in action by living not only for ourselves but for all creatures and for God, is the highest type of sacrifice. Awareness of our relationship with the primal source of all being must be expressed in sacrifice—in our compassionate devotion to the welface of all men and creatures, of all beings (sarva-bhūta-hita). To do so is to find Truth, for the absolute good of all beings is Truth. Yad bhūta hitaṁ atyantaṁ tat satyaṁ iti dhāraṇā.[62] Those who do not realize this are, as the *Taittirīya Brāhmaṇa* says, infatuated with rites performed with the help of fire, and choked by smoke, they neither know the world in which they live, nor the spirit.[63]

Upaniṣads

In the Upaniṣads we find three attitudes towards sacrifices and rituals: (1) Strict and correct performance of them purifies the mind and makes one fit for the knowledge of Brahman.[64] (2) One need not perform the sacrifices physically; it is not only enough but better to enagage oneself in meditations concerning the sacrifices as given in the scriptures.[65] (3) The fruits of sacrifices are impermanent, the wise man discards them and seeks only saving knowledge.[66] I will now develop these three themes.

(1) When actions such as the daily study of the Veda and sacrifices prescribed by the scriptures are performed as duties which one ought to do and not because of the rewards they confer, they serve to purify the mind and make it fit for the reception of saving truth. A man of this type will not engage himself in rituals and sacrifices which are intended only for obtaining special benefits. He will concern himself only with "regular rites', such as prayer, charity, the five great sacrifices and askesis, i.e., dispassionate enjoyment of sense-objects.[67] Duty performed as duty without motivated by the good that results therefrom purifies the

mind. Any action that purifies is a sacrifice *Eṣa vai yajño yo'yaṁ pavate.*[68]

(2) A better way of performing a sacrifice than to do it physically is to undertake a particular type of meditation concerning it.[69] Thus, for example, instead of performing the horse-sacrifice, one can meditate upon the universe as a sacrificial horse. The dawn is its head, the sun its eye, time its body, and so on everything in the universe is meditated upon as a limb of the horse sacrificed for Prajāpati. Prajāpati imagined himself as a great sacrificial animal, and sacrificed it to himself because he wanted to make a sacrifice. In a similar way one can now imagine oneself as well as the whole world as a sacrificial animal and meditate thus: While being sanctified with mantras I am dedicated to the gods, and while being killed for myself, all animals are sacrificed to me, for I represent Prajāpati, of whom the gods are parts.[70] Or, to take another example, a person's whole life may symbolically be meditated upon as a Soma sacrifice. Dividing one's life into three portions, each can be imagined as a soma libation. Whenever a man suffers privations, hungers or thirsts, he is undergoing the initiatory consecration; whenever he eats and drinks, laughs and enjoys he joins in the Upasada and stuta-śastra ceremonies in which these are allowed; when he procreates, he is reborn; when he dies he takes the final bath after the sacrifice. Practice of austerity, charity and truthfulness are the gifts he makes in this life-long soma sacrifice.[71] Or, to give another example, this world is fire, earth its fuel, fire its smoke, night its flame, moon its cinder, and the stars its sparks. In this fire gods offer rain and thereby food is produced. Man is fire, in whom the gods offer food, from which arises further life.[72] And the last example: The Supreme Self is in oneself, all that one eats is an offering to that. To meditate so is to perform the agnihotra sacrifice.[73] Any kind of offering, and all self-restraint (*saṁyamana*) are unending and immortal sacrifices. He who knows this, says the *Kauṣītakī*, is sacri-

ficing continuously and uninterruptedly, whether waking or sleeping.[74]

The meditation the Upaniṣads prescribe, it is argued, is based on correct understanding, it is not like regarding a post as a man. It is similar to meditating upon an image as God, knowing that the image is not God, but that it could be an aid to meditation. In other words, the image is a symbol of God and by meditation on it we rise to a fuller knowledge of God. It is just a means, a ladder for our spiritual ascent. Similarly, by meditating upon the world as a sacrificial animal, or human life as one continuous sacrifice, one gains access to spiritual truth. Also, for those who take the scriptures to be true and infallible, such meditations take on a sacramental character. They are interior symbolizations of something sacred, efficacious of well-being. Only in a figurative sense is an image God, and when we say that God has that or this attribute, we are then too indulging in metaphorical statements, for the true God "has" nothing, but is infinite and perfect Being. So though the world is not a sacrificial horse, yet such a meditation is conducive to well-being, giving the same fruit which is got by an actual sacrifice, and moreover it enables one to apprehend through this symbol a spiritual truth.[75]

On the basis of certain Vedic texts like the following the late U. Ganapati Sastri (1888-1989), a renowned Vedic scholar, held that the study and recitation (pārāyaṇa) of śruti passages describing sacrifices would have the very same results as their performance would have. In other words, performance of sacrifices and pārāyaṇa of the Vedic portions dealing with them have identical effect: Yaṁ yaṁ kratumadhīte tena tenāsyeṣṭam bhavati". Svādhyāya (study and repetition) and pravacana (teaching or discoursing on) of the Veda, Sastri quoted, is indeed tapas (askesis). "Svādhyāyapravacane eveti nāko Maudgalyaḥ, taddhi tapastaddhitapaḥ". (*Taittirīya śruti*)

(3) Finally, to revert back to the attitude of the Upaniṣads. They disparage the actual ritualistic sacrifices, not be-

cause they do not confer upon the sacrificer the fruits promised by the Veda, but because these are impermanent. They can give us only prosperity in this world, or happiness in the other, but cannot give us liberation. One may go to heaven as a result of the merit acquired by good deeds and sacrifices, but when that merit is exhausted, one has to be reborn in this world. There is a higher end for man than the acquisition of merit and enjoyment in heaven, and that is union with the Imperishable Person. This true salvation is to be gained by askesis, faith and renunciation; there is no salvation through works. By what one does one cannot attain Brahman; only by what one knows and believes can one win the Immortal.[76]

The Upaniṣadic teaching may be summed up thus. Actual sacrifices and ritual have no great spiritual value, although they do give the results which scriptures speak of. So they should be discarded. But there are some actions, e.g., the five mahāyajñas and daily duties, which are not for selfish individual ends, but for the good of all. Performance of them as duty which is an end in itself purifies a man and makes him a worthy vessel of salvation. Meditation concerning the sacrifices, to conceive the world or life as a sacrificial act, is of greater value than actual performance of them. It takes on a sacramental character, and develops spiritual insight. This prepares the way for the vision of Brahman, which is the ultimate end of human life.*

He who does not lead a sacrificial life lives in vain. (*Gītā*, III. 16).

* The above account of yajña is drawn from my book *The Realm of Between*, Simla, 1973, ch. III.

IV
THE MEANING OF THE VEDA

There is a sūkta in the *Ṛgveda,* X. 71, entitled "Jñānaṁ".[+] The second and third lines of its first verse are: "Out of love the seers revealed the best and purest deeply hidden in their hearts". Yadeṣāṁ śreṣṭhaṁ yadaripramāsīt preṇā tadeṣām nihitaṁ guhāviḥ. In the *Atharvaveda* (IV. I.) there is a sūkta with the title "Brahmavidyā", and the second and third lines of its first verse are: "The seer disclosed the different aspects of Brahman, the holy utterance and what is meant by it, which is the source of both the existent and non-existent". Sa budhnyā upamā asya viṣṭhāḥ sataśca yonimasatasca vi vaḥ. *Ṛgveda,* I. 164.39, says: "all the gods have been occupying the supreme position, namely the eternal syllable of the Veda. What will one, who does not know it, do with the Veda? Those who know it sit together". Yastanna veda kim ṛcā kariṣyati? Ya it tad vidusta ime samāsate.

*

A Ṛgvedic text asserts that the great *asuratva,* energy or strength, of all the gods is one only. Mahad devānāṁ asuratvamekaṁ.[77] There is the famous line in its first maṇḍala itself which declares, "The sages call the One Real in many ways".[78] Ekaṁ sad viprā bahudhā vadanti. This is repeated in the last maṇḍala also: "The sages imagine and describe the One Being variously".[79] Viprāḥ kavayo vacobhiḥ ekaṁ santaṁ bahudhā kalpayanti. In another context a graphic description of Divine Unity is found: "The one fire kindled in many ways burns at different places, the one all-pervading Sun illumines the universe, the one Dawn lights up all

---

[+] Sāyaṇa remarks that this sūkta praises the knowledge of the Supreme Brahman, which is the means for man's highest end. Earlier, the *Bṛhaddevatā* stated the same.

this earth, the One only has become all this which exists".[80] Ekaṁ vā idaṁ vi babhūva sarvaṁ.

Similarly, the Yajurveda asserts: "He is Agni, He is Āditya"; "Only by knowing Him one goes beyond death, there is no other path for that".[81] He is the Self-born who taught people truths exactly as they are through overlasting years.[82]

The last Veda, the *Atharva*, penetrates even deeper into Divine Unity and the inseparable togetherness or identity (?) of man and Deity.

(1) Its "Ucchiṣṭa Brahmasūkta" declares: What remains after all that is empirical is considered to be taken away is the 'Remnant Absolute' (Ucchiṣṭa Brahman). In it is set together the whole world, heaven and earth, all existence, all the gods, being and non-being; and from it come all gods and men; all that happened, happens or will happen occurs in it. The wise consider the human being as Brahman, as in him all the gods dwell. He is the abode of gods.[83] (Vidvān puruṣamidaṁ Brahmeti manyate. Gṛhaṁ kṛtvā martyaṁ devāḥ puruṣaṁ āviśan.)

(2) In its "Sarvādhāravarṇanaṁ" this Veda attempts to find a transcendental principle which is the Skambha (Support) of everything, as it sustains everything. "Whoever knows Brahman in man (ye puruṣe Brahma viduḥ) knows the highest One, and accordingly the Skambha".[84]

(3) In the "Jyeṣṭhabrahmavarṇanaṁ", He who lords over the past, present and future and everything, who alone is transcendent, is called the Principal Absolute (Jyeṣṭha Brahma). He is ever-lasting and ever-renewed. All that moves, all that sustains the earth,—is the combined one. He is the unageing beautiful one, the immortal in mortal abode. He is woman, man, boy, girl, and the aged one who totters. He is the string of the string in which all these created beings are woven. The Brahman-knowers know the mysterious spiritual entity (yakṣa) within the human body. It is free from desire, wise, immortal, self-existent, content with

(its own) essence (rasena tṛptaḥ) and perfect. Knowing that wise, unageing, youthful Self as one's own self, one is not afraid of death, (Akāmo dhīro amṛtaḥ svayambhūḥ . . . ajaraṁ yuvānaṁ.)[85]

(4) In another sūkta, the *Atharvaveda* informs us that the one who intensely longs beholds in secret the highest in which everything becomes uniform. (yatra viśvam bhavatyekarūpaṁ.)

The *Atharvaveda* describes Brahman not only as Skambha, Jyeṣṭha, etc., but even as a *vrātya.* A vrātya is a vagrant, a non-initiated, or a violator of social norm and decency.[86]

As already cited, not only the saṁhitās, even the brāhmaṇas assert that the Supreme Self is worshipped by different names in different ways. He unites all.[87] The Āraṇyakas say that the same principle present in all is called Brahman;[88] and that it is what the followers of the Ṛgveda, Yajurveda and Sāmaveda meditate upon in different ways.[89]

In the context which starts with: "The Self alone was in the beginning", in the course of its exposition the *Bṛhadāraṇyaka* says: "When people talk of particular gods thus, "worship this one" or "worship that one" they are talking of His projections only, because this one (the Self) alone is all the gods".[90] Eṣa u hyeva sarve devāḥ. He is the Law; he only is today and tomorrow also.[91] The *Muṇḍaka Upaniṣad* says that all the gods, men and animals are born in various ways from the divine formless Person beyond the highest immutable.[92] In Brahman, the *Kaṭha* declares, all the gods are established, and no one transcends it.[93] That Great Thing is the meaning of the Veda; he who does not know that meaning does not know It.[94] Nāvedavinmanute taṁ bṛhantaṁ.

NOTES

1. *Śrīmadbhāgavata,* IX. 14.48.
2. *Ibid.,* II. 7.36: "Vedadrumaṁ viṭapaśo vibhajiṣyati." *Mahābhārata,* crit. edn., I.57.73: "Vivyāsa Vedān yasmācca tasmād vyāsa iti smṛtaḥ".
3. *Śatapatha Brāhmaṇa,* I.7.1.5: "Yajño vai śreṣṭhatamam karma".
4. *Chāndogya,* I.3.4: "Yā ṛk tatsāma"; and I.6.1: "Ṛci adhyūḍham sāma".
5. His *Atharvaveda-bhāṣya-bhūmikā*: "Sarvasāratvād ayaṁ vedaḥ śreṣṭhaḥ".
6. *Gopatha Brāhmaṇa,* III.2: "Atharvāṅgirobhiḥ brahmatvaṁ". Also, II.24.
7. *Ibid.,* I.4.
8. e.g., Agnirjāto Atharvaṇā", *Ṛgveda,* X.21.5. "Yajñairatharvā prathamaḥ pathastate", *op.cit.,* I.83.5. *Vājasaneyī Yajurveda,* XI.32: "Atharvā tvā prathamo viramanthadagne".
9. *Chāndogya,* III.4.1-2. *Bṛhadāraṇyaka,* IV.4.10. *Taittirīya,* III.i. *Muṇḍaka,* I.1.
10. On "Catvāri śṛṅgā (Ṛg., IV.58.6:) *Nirukta Pari.* I.7. says, "Vedā vā ete uktāḥ"; and Patañjali says, "Catvāro Vedā eva catvāri śṛṅgāṇi".
11. *Ṛgveda,* I. 164.46; X.114.5.
12. *Ibid.,* X. 129.2.
13. *Ibid.,* X.164.39. "Ya ittadvidusta ime samāsate". "Apunarāvṛttyā svarūpevasthānaṁ samāsanam", Sāyaṇa. Samāsanaṁ muktiḥ, Ātmānanda. For same idea, Ṛg., I.65.1., etc.
14. The *Yajurveda* begins, "Devo vaḥ savitā prārpayatu śreṣṭhatamāya karmaṇā apyāyadhvaṁ"; reminds "puruṣam mahāntaṁ . . . tameva viditvā . . . nānyaḥ panthāḥ"; and concludes, "Īśāvāsyamidaṁ".
15. III.3.1. "Sāmaveda eva puṣpaṁ."
16. See note 4 above.
17. *Mīmāṁsā Sūtra,* 2.1.36.
18. The gati of Sāmans is svara, *Chāndogya,* I.8.4.
19. Sāmnaḥ : "Tasya svara eva svaṁ, "*Bṛhadāraṇyaka,* I.3.25.
20. *Ṛgveda,* VIII.98.1.
21. *Atharva,* XV.6.9.
22. *Atharva,* X.7.17: X.8.43.
23. "Śāntikapuṣṭikādipratiṣṭhāhetukarmapradhānatvāt, "*Taittirīya-bhāṣya,* II.3.1.
24. Sāyaṇa Bhāṣya on *Ṛgveda,* I.164.39: "Sarvairvedaiḥ khalu Brahma adhigamyate. . . . Buddhiśuddhyutpādanadvārā vedanasādhanatvena Brahmaviṣayatvaṁ bhaviṣyati.
25. Ātmānanda's Bhāṣya in C. Kunhan Raja, *Asya Vāmasya Hymn,* Text with two bhāṣyas, trans., & notes, Madras, 1956, pp.16, 77. "Sarvepi vedo Brahmātmaikyo-viṣayaḥ."
26. 'Avibhāgena; Bhāṣya on *Kaṭha,* I.2.15

27. IV.4.10.
28. IV.4.22. "Ātmaviṣaye sarvo vedo upayukto bhavati." "Evaṁ karmakāṇḍenāsyaikavākyatāvagatiḥ."
29. *Vedārthasaṅgraha*, 231: "Vedāḥ Parabrahmabhūta-Nārāyaṇasvarūpaṁ tadārādhanaprakāram ārādhitāt phalaviśeṣaṁ ca bodhayanti."
30. Citations: "Vede ... Viṣṇuḥ sarvatra gīyate. Viṣṇuparā eva sarve Vedāḥ. Viṣṇau Vedāḥ pratiṣṭhitāḥ."
31. *Śrutisūktimālikā, Caturveda-tātparyasaṅgraha*, ślokas 2-3. "Mantrārthavādavidhibhirbahudhāvibhakto, yaśśabdarāśiranapekṣatayā pramāṇaṁ, so'yaṁ vimatsaravimṛṣṭapadārthatattvo Vedaḥ prakāśayati kevalamīśvaraṁ tvām".
32. *The Religion of the Veda*, New York, 1908, p.51.
33. *Religions of Ancient India*, London, 1953, p.26-27, 18.
34. For reference, see my book mentioned in n.2 of Chapter II.
35. Pratyakṣeṇānumityā vā yastūpāyo na buddhyate, enaṁ vidanti Vedena tasmādvedasya Vedatā".
36. Aditi confessed to Kṛṣṇa that she was unfortunately guilty in having worshipped Him not for liberation, but for the victory of her sons over their enemies. This, she said, was like desiring from the kalpadruma a piece of cloth enough to cover the pudendum. Kaupīnācchādanaprāyā vāñcchā kalpadrumādapi. (Her prayer to Kṛṣṇa when he went to her after killing Naraka. *Viṣṇupurāṇa*).
37. *Bṛhadāraṇyaka*, VI.6.4.18f. "Atha ya icchetputro me paṇḍito vigītaḥ", etc.
38. For the idea that creation is sacrifice: *Ṛgveda*, X. 72, 81, 82, 90 etc.
39. *Ṛgveda*, X.31.2.
40. *Ṛgveda*, VIII.32.16.
41. *Ṛg*, II.35.12.
41a. *Ṛg*, X.63.12; VIII. 70.11.
42. *Ṛg*, X.88.8. Fire seems to be an ancient medium, VIII.102.10. It is gods' tongue through which they taste oblations (X.65).
43. *Ṛg*, X.90
44. *Śatapatha*, XIV.3.2.1.
45. *Op.cit.*, IX. 4.1.11.
46. Cp. *Taittirīya Saṁhitā*, VII.2.4.1.
47. *Śatapatha*, I.2.2.9; VII.2.9.
48. Ibid., XI.1.8.2-5; III.6.2. 16; I.7.2.1-6.
49. *Pañcaviṁśa*, V.6.10; *Taitirīya Saṁhitā*, VI.I. 11.6.
50. *Śatapatha*, I.2.3.6.
51. *Ibid.*, X.5.2.20.
52. III.2.3.9.
53. *Śatapatha*, XI. 5.6.1. Cp. *Taittirīya Āraṇyaka*: "Pañca vā ete mahāyajñāḥ satati pratayante". *Chāndogya Pariśiṣṭa*: Mahāsattrāṇi

jānīyāt ta eva hi mahāmakhāḥ". also, *Manusmṛti*, III. 68-71. A sattra is a sacrificial session extending from twelve nights to a thousand years (usually a chain of soma sacrifices) intended to remove 'darkness'. "Na asya (tamasaḥ) anyena sattrāt apaghāto'sti". (*Śatapatha*, XI.5.5.1.)

54. "Yajñamahāyajñau vyaṣṭisamaṣṭisambandhāt", says Aṅgirā. "Samaṣṭisambandhānmahayajñāḥ", says Bharadvāja.
55. *Gītā*, II.50: Yoga is skill in action.
56. *Śatapatha*, XI.5.7.1. Paktiḥ=paripākaḥ (Sāyaṇa). Loka is either the "people" or "the world".
57. See the Vedic texts: "Niṣkārano vedo'dhyeyo jñeyaśca; yo hi vidyām adhītya arthine na brūyāt sa kāryahā syāt śreyaso dvāraṁ apāvṛṇuyāt".
58. II.118.
59. "Annaṁ bhūmau śvacaṇḍālavāyasebhyaśca nikṣipet", says *Yājñavalkya Smṛti*.
60. *Manusmṛti*, III. 68f.
61. *Ṛg Veda*, X.117.6: "Kevalāgho bhavati kevalādī".
62. *Mahābhārata*, Vana, 208.4. Also Śānti, 329.13; 28.19.
63. III. X.2.1.
64. *Muṇḍaka* 3.2.10; *Śvetāśvatara*, II. 6; *Bṛhadāraṇyaka*, IV. 4.22.
65. Meditation and rites are alternatives, says the *Śatapatha*, X.IV. 3.9.; and the *Taittirīya Saṁhitā*, V. III. 12.2.
66. *Muṇḍaka*, I.2.7.10.
67. *Bṛhadāraṇyaka*, IV. 4.22, and Śaṅkara's commentary on it. Also, *Muṇḍaka*, III. 1.8. Cp. *Śatapatha*, XI. II. VI. 13.
68. IV.16.1.
69. In his Bhāṣya on *Bṛhadāraṇyaka*, I.1., Śaṅkara makes it clear that meditation is not part of a rite, but an alternative to it. It produces a greater result than mere ritual.
70. *Bṛhadāraṇyaka*, I.1. & 2. Śaṅkara on Ibid., I. 2.7.
71. *Chāndogya*, III.16.
72. *Bṛhadāraṇyaka*, VI. 2.11-12.
73. *Chāndogya*, V. 19-24.
74. *Kauṣītakī*, II.5.
75. Śaṅkara on *Bṛhadāraṇyaka*, I. 3.1.
76. *Muṇḍaka*, I.2.
77. III. 55.1.
78. I.164.46.
79. X. 114.4.
80. VIII. 58.2.
81. XXXII. 1., XXX.18.
82. 40.8.
83. XI. 7-8.

84. X.7.
85. X.8.
86. *Cūlikā Upaniṣad*, quoted by Whitney, *Atharvaveda Saṁhitā*, HOS, Vol. II, p. 769.
87. *Śatapatha*, X. 5.2.20.
88. *Taittirīya Āraṇyaka*, III.2.3.9.
89. *Aitareya Āraṇyaka*, III. 2.3.12. Etaṁ hyeva bahvṛcā mahatyukthe mīmāṁsanta etamagnavadhvaryava etaṁ mahāvrate chandogāḥ.
90. I.4.6.
91. I.6.5.
92. II.1.1-7.
93. II.1.9. (Arpitāḥ=pratiṣṭhitāḥ, Rāmānuja).
94. *Śāṭyāyanopaniṣad* 4; *Itihāsopaniṣad*, 20.

IDEA BEHIND JACKET DESIGN

Aitareya Upaniṣad (1.ii, 4) says "Agnirvāg bhūtvā mukhaṁ prāviśat". So the Śruti-interpreters' speech is represented by fire-flames. The *handing down* of the oral Vedārthamīmāṃsā tradition is also nicely captured by the *spreading* of fire "pravartito dipa iva pradīpāt"—as Kālidāsa said!

However, the interpreter is not merely uttering *words*, but wishes to unveil Truth. And, of course, truth is paradigmatically represented by the Sun: tattvaṁ pūṣaṇ apāvruṇu satyadharmāya dṛṣṭaye (*Iśa*, 14). Hence, through *closed* eyes (not "open" towards the outer objects: parāñci khāni vyatruṇat svayambhūḥ—the outward senses would not see the pratyagātman—so the eyes are closed to the world but open inwardly!) when the interpreter meditates on the Sun of truth (notice the *Sun* in Plato's Parable of the Cave), the *fire* of *words* comes out from his mouth which is what śrutyarthaparyālocanaṁ promises to be!

—Dr. Arindam Chakrabarty

The author is grateful to Dr. Arindam Chakrabarty for his thoughtful jacket design.

Index

Abhinava Gupta 56
Abhyūha 28
Action, real sacrificial 54
Action, renunciation of or yoga of 65
Action, sacrifices spring from 54
Action, skill in 85
Ādityasena 35
Ailuṣa, Kavaṣa 14
Aitareya, Mahīdāsa 15
Aitiśāyana 17
Ajāmila 47
Akṣara 28
Al-Biruni 7fn
Allchin, F.R. 78
Ānantya 43, 45
Anvaya-vyatireka 32
Āpadeva 36
Apalā 15
Āpastamba 2
Āpta 28fn
Arjuna 54
Arthavādas 1fn, 2
Ārya Samājists 17
Aśvattha 55fn
Ātmānanda 11, 76
Ātmanastuṣṭi 62
Audumbarāyaṇa 12
Aupamanyava 12
Aurobindo, Sri 2, 11 17
Authority, Vedas as 44
Authority, Vedic 63

Bādarāyaṇa 17
Bādari 17
Bergaigne, Abel 26
Bhagavadgītā 62, 75
Bhagavadgītā, karmayoga of 40
Bhakti 79
Bhakti-yoga 48
Bharadvāja 85
Bhartṛmitra 36
Bhāṣya, Sāyaṇa's 10
Bhāṣya, Veṅkaṭa-Mādhava's 10
Bhoja, king 35
Bhūtayajña 85, 86
Bloomfield, Maurice 77
Bṛahddevatā, Śaunaka's 10, 13
Brahmā 5
Brahman 3, 4, 79
Brahman, knowledge of 79
Brahman, Supreme 77
Brahman, the paths to 45
Brahman, *Oṁ Tat Sat* as the threefold designation of 55
Brāhmaṇas 2
Brahman-knowledge 34, 51
Brahma-sūtra 53
Brahmavādinaḥ 56fn
Brahmayajña 16, 85
Brāhmin 41
Brāhmin, true 43

Caitanya 56
Cārvī 57
Chāndasas 35
Chanting, Vedic 7
Criteria, six 23, 76fn

Dasgupta, S.N. 31
Deity, sacrifices as acts of pleasing 82
Desire 39
Devayajña 85
Dharma 3, 34
Dharma, fourfold character of 62
Dharma, śruti as the authority for 40
Dharma, Vaidika 63
Dharma, Veda as not the sole

source of 62
Dharma and Brahman, Veda as what makes known 80
Dharmarāja 23
Dīkṣita, Appayya 77
Dīrghatamas 15
Discussion (vāda) 58
Dissolution, creation and 80
'Domination of the initial passage', principle of 24
Dravya-yajña 51
Durgācārya 29
Duties, obligatory regular 78

Effects, injunctions and prohibitions have no moral (a view) 57
Eligible, Śūdras are 17
Eternal, Veds is not (a view) 38
Ethics 4
Existence, struggle for 86

Fearless 49fn.
'Fifth Veda', *Mahābhārata* as 46
Fundamentalism, Vedic 61

Gārgī 15
Gauḍapāda 32
Geldner, Karl 27
Gibberish, Veda contains only (a view) 57
Gītā 51, 52, 53, 54, 56, 65
Goal, ultimate 49
God 38
God, dedication of the fruits of actions to 78
God, glorification of the One 10
God, knowledge of 4
God, One 53
Gods, Vedic 10
Good, supreme 39
Good, the
Govindarāja 46
Grammar, purpose of 37

Gṛhasthas 45
Guṇas, three 50

Hanūmān 57
Haradattaśivācārya 77
Householder (gṛhastha) 42

Imperishable 55
Incantations, Veda a collection of (a view) 57
Inference 4
Interpretation, monotheistic 11
Interpretation, ritualistic 10
Intuition 3

Jābāli 57fn
Jābāli, Satyakāma 15
Jaimini 17, 75
Jalpa 58
Janaśruti 15
Jayatīrtha 11
Jñāna-yajña 51
Jñāneśvara 56

Kaiyaṭa 16
Kakṣīvān 14, 15
Kālidāsa 81
Kapila 37, 42, 43, 44, 45
Karmayoga, Vedic 39, 40
Kātyāyana 1
Kautsa 35
Kautsa's theory 36
Keith, A.B. 25
Knowledge, Vedāntic systems the ultimate source of saving 59
Kṛṣṇa 54
Kumārila 31, 36, 78

Lokavidviṣṭa dharma 62
Lokaviruddha action 62
Lokāyatas 57
Lopāmudrā 15
Lüders 78

Madhvācārya 33, 77
Mahābhārata 62, 63, 64
Mahāyajñas, five 90
Mahāyajñas, Śūdras are eligible to perform the five 16
Maitreyī 15
Manana 31
Mantras 1fn, 2
Mantras, 'gods' have no existence apart from (a view) 36
Mantras, theory of the meaninglessness (ānarthakya) of 35
Mantras, Vedic 12
Manusmṛti 60, 62
Manuṣyayajña 85
Means, 'Ānuśravika' 37
Mīmāṁsā 5, 59
Mīmāṁsā, importance of 31
Modesty 45
Morality, meaninglessness of (a view) 57
Murāri 26

Nāgeśa 16
Name, 'god' is only a (a view) 36
Nārāyaṇa 77
Nididhyāsana 32
Nīlakaṇṭha 11
Nirāmaya 43
Niṣkāma karma (desireless action) 59
Non-arrogance 45
Non-injury 40, 45
Non-malice 45
Non-sacrificer 42
Nyāya 5, 58

Oṁ 56

Pāṇini 2, 81
Pāraskara 35
Pārthasārathi Miśra 36
Patañjali 5, 74
Patience 45
Peace 45
Perception 3
Person, Supreme 55
Person, surrender to the Supreme 46
Pischel, Richard 27
Pitṛyajña 85
Prabhākara 2, 78
Prajāpati 84
Precepts, conflict of Vedic 53
Principal Absolute (Jyeṣṭha Brahma) 92
Propitiation, rituals as acts of 10
Purport 23
Puruṣa 83
Puruṣamedha 61fn

Rāghavendra 11
Raikva 15
Rāmānanda 56
Rāmānujācārya 33, 51, 77, 79
Ram Gopal 25
Reason 60
Reason, one's own 53
Reasoning (tarka) 58
Reductio ad absurdum 58
Relinquishment 40
'Remnant Absolute' (Ucchiṣṭa Brahman) 92
Renou, Louis 59, 78
Renunciation, askesis, faith and 90
Ṛgveda 73, 74
Ṛgveda, the main purpose of 75
Rituals, three attitudes towards sacrifices and 87
Roth, principle of 26

Sacrifice 84
Sacrifice, highest type of 87
Sacrifices 54
Sacrifices, bloody 61
Sacrifices, five 85
Sacrifices, five great 85

Sacrifices, symbolic explanations of 11
Śākapūṇi 12
Śālikanātha 31
Samādhi (enstatis) 59
Śama 40fn
Sāmans 75
Sāmaveda 74, 75
Sāṁkhya 59
Saṁnyāsa 65
Sanatsujāta 41
Śaṅkara 2, 32, 52, 53, 76
Śaṅkarācārya 4, 31, 33, 51
Sarasvatī, Madhusūdana 2, 3, 32
Saraswati, Swami Dayananda 2, 9, 11
Sarvamedha 61fn
Śāstra 53
Śāstra, *Gītā* as a 53
Śāstras *par excellence*, Vedas as 53
Sastri, U. Ganapati 89
Sastri, Mm. A. Chinnaswami 25
Sastry, T.V. Kapali 2, 11
Sat 56
Sāyaṇa 1, 2, 3, 12, 13, 26, 34, 74, 83
Scripture 6, 33
Scripture, Veda as a universal 14
Self, knowledge of 39
Self, Supreme 84
Self-rule (svārājya) 39
Sense-control 40
Shikoh, Prince Dara 17
Sincerity 45
Śiva 77
Skacel, Jan 28
Skambha (support) 92
Smṛti, *Gītā* as a 53
Source, Veda as an eternal and infallible 3
Śravaṇa 31
Śrīkaṇṭhācārya 77
Śrotriyas 35
Straightforwardness 45
Śūdras 14, 17
Śūdras, Anirvasita 16
Sūkta, Puruṣa 83
Sureśvara 31
Symbolizations, interior 89
Syūmaraśmi, dialogue between Kapila and 42

Tapas 40fn
Tarka 31, 32
Tarka, the place of 58
Tat 56
Tātparya 22
Tātparya, definition of 23
Tattvajñāna 58
THAT 76
THOU 76
Tolerance 45
Tranquillity 45
Truth 40, 45, 47
Truth, sense perception and infer-ence can be the sources of 57
Tyāga 40fn, 65
Tyāgarāja 7
Types, divine and demonic 52

Upanayana, Śūdras can receive 16
Uvaṭa 25

Vācaspati 31, 32
Vaiśeṣika 59
Varāhamihira 81
Veda, definition of 2, 3
Veda, eternal or produced 37
Veda, hymns of primitives ? 25
Veda, polytheistic interpretation of 10
Veda, Supreme Self as source of the 80
Veda, fifth 40

Veda, Upaniṣadic portion of 3
Veda, apauruṣeyatva of 80
Veda, Atharva 74, 75
Veda, *Atharvāṅgirasa* 74
Veda, *Bhṛgvaṅgirasa* 74
Vedānta 5
Vedapāṭha 34
Vedapāṭhakas 35
Vedastuti 48
Vedavāda 49, 50
Vedaviruddha actions 62
Vedic action, twofold 39
Vedic ritualism, mechanical performance of 54
Vedic study, tabu on 17
Vedic study, women eligible for 15
Vedic tree, the flower of the 54
Veṅkaṭa-Mādhava 25, 35
Vibhūti 75
Vidhis 2
Vimarśa 53fn
Viṣṇu 77
Vitaṇḍā 58
Viveka (discrimination) 59
Vivekananda, Swami 17
Vṛtra legend 11
Vyākaraṇa 58
Vyāsa 73

Whitney 26
Women, eligibility of 17
Worship, sacrifice as an act of 82

Yājñavalkya 62
Yajurveda 73, 74
Yajurveda, Śukla 75
Yakṣa 92
Yāska 2, 5, 10, 12, 13, 34, 74, 92
Yatis 43

100 YEARS

मोतीलाल बनारसीदास
सैद मिठा
बाजार
लाहौर

1903

MOTILAL B
PUBL